Faces
What You See is What You Get

Dedication

In memory of my parents, J. B. and Ruth Moore.
And for my aunt, Norma Curtis Hood,
who always believed in me.

Faces

What You See is What You Get

A Guide to Reading People
Immediately and Accurately

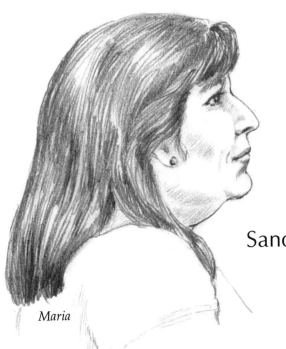

Maria

Written and illustrated by

Sandra Moore Williams

Que Publishing Services

Illustrations by Sandra Moore Williams. Book designed and produced by Que Publishing Services, P.O. Box 24911, Fort Worth, TX 76124-1911

Find us on the Web at: http://www. onthemarkfacereading.com

Library of Congress Cataloging-in-Publication Data

Williams, Sandra Moore

      Faces: What You See is What You Get: A Guide to Reading the Personality
         Traits on a Face

    Includes topical index

    ISBN 0-9742140-1-9

    1. Physiognomy. I. Title

    2. Self-help

Zak

ACKNOWLEDGEMENTS

I wish to acknowledge those friends of mine who believed I really could write a book and actively encouraged me: Satya Chase, Diane Siegel, Cheryl Malone, Charles Riley, Debra Baker, Milli Thornton, Bette Epstein, and Dan Chick. I might not have gotten this far this soon without them and I thank them from the bottom of my heart. My special thanks to Rebekah Mercer, Ina Crowe, and my daughter, Heather Beverly, whose sharpened pencils brought clarity to some fuzzy places. Others who have borne with me through this process and/or helped me in myriad ways include Shari Stament, Sallie Buck, and Rob Bliss.

All areas of study owe some recognition to those whose work helped create a foundation that others build upon, I truly appreciate all those face readers who have gone before me and shared the legacy of their observations, theories, and conclusions, especially Mac Fulfer and Naomi Tickle. My thanks also to my many clients and students who understand the value of what I do and the thousands of people whose faces I have read, many of whom gave me valuable feedback helping me more deeply understand what's behind a face. I salute all of you.

Karl

TRAIT INDEX

Face Traits

CONTENTS

Olga

Faces like the one above were designed to be both illustrative and instructive. Practice your reading skills on them as you learn the traits, then check the accuracy of your reading by turning to the "Faces: the Trait Readouts," page 165.

INTRODUCTION:
WHY READ FACES?

She walked up to my booth at a trade show, stopped, hands on her hips, and studied my sign, "Face Reading, the Instant Personality Profile." Then she looked straight at me with a skeptical smile and challenged, "What *is* this?"

"A personality profile based on the structure and proportions of your face." I said.

"That's all?"

"What were you expecting?"

"I already know my personality. Why would anyone want to do this?"

"People have different reasons," I began, "however *you* might do it because your face shows you are unafraid of new things, you're curious, and you have an insatiable need to know *why*. In fact, "why" is probably your favorite word. You probe and question everything, especially if it doesn't seem to fit with your mind set. Those eyes show an incredible need to have everything make sense from your point of view. I would expect you even badger people about their views to bring them around to a more "reasonable" approach, which of course, means more like yours."

"Omigosh!" She stopped me and reaching into her purse, pulled out the appropriate sum, and plopping it on the table, sat down. "You are totally accurate so far. And tell me, how does this work and where does it come from and how did you learn it?"

She's not alone in her curiosity about face reading. The idea that the face might hold clues about the underlying person, their motivations, habitual thought patterns, and behaviors is an idea that has intrigued many great minds for centuries. *(For a brief history of face reading in Western culture, see Appendix A, "Face Reading Time Line," page 160.)*

Form, Function, and History

In nature, science has found that form follows function. All life forms are examples; such as the anteater whose snout and tongue are specifically formed for the function of extracting and eating ants. Or the hummingbird with a beak for sucking nectar and a body that allows it to hover over flowers. You get the idea.

The question is, how far can you take this form/function concept, especially with regard to the human personality? Yes, we all have eyes in front so we have good depth perception. We all have teeth suited to eating a variety of foods and we all have rather flat faces instead of a long muzzle like a dog or herbivore. Yet within that basic structure of the human face, each is unique. Certainly people don't think or act exactly alike. So, do these two facts have any relationship to each other? Do the variations in structure have any relevance to the variations in behavior?

Thinkers have researched the concept, advanced theories and created systems for reading faces, with the first recorded use by the Greek philosopher and mathematician, Pythagoras, in the sixth century BC. It is reputed that he used a system of face reading as an essential part of his student interview process and accordingly turned away young men he deemed unsuitable for his school. (He was also probably the first person to be assassinated for his conclusions about a face reading subject* — and let's hope the last!) The concept has endured through the centuries with various approaches, purposes and conclusions.

Some of the more important advances in research were conducted in the last century by the late Judge Edward V. Jones of Los Angeles. His enduring contributions included addressing his theories in light of the brain mapping, genetic and physiologic research that was being published at the time (circa 1920—1950). He hypothesized that the traits were universal and demonstrated varying degrees of strength, with the physical indicators being proportional rather than simple anatomical points.[1]

Aside from the material handed down through the centuries from various theorists, other face reading systems have been developed by several proponents largely from an anecdotal or intuitive approach. Chinese face reading, called *Siang Mien*, has been practiced for over 3000 years. It is employed as a form of divination as well as character reading. I have studied several of these schools of thought, and in this book I offer the integration of much of what I have learned through study, informal research, and personal experience.

The renowned philosopher was murdered by a vindictive, would-be student who was refused acceptance into Pythagoras' school of esoteric studies. Pythagoras read the faces of all applicants and one would assume he saw characteristics he didn't like on this one, and apparently with good reason.

1. Whiteside, Bill, *Nature's Message*, DeHarts, 2000

Reading Faces as an Aid to Communication

One of the greatest benefits of reading faces is the understanding it can bring to the communication process. When you know how a person processes information and have a general idea of how they are predisposed to view their world, it becomes much easier to tailor your communications to that person as your "target audience" of one. A basic fact of life is that we lack understanding of people who are very unlike us. In some ways, they really do speak a different language and there can be a definite communication barrier.

To be effective in your communications, you need to be able to cut through the differences and "speak their language." In the study of face reading, you learn your own trait characteristics as well as how to "talk to the traits" you see on other people, so you understand what other people need and want from you. In the process, you learn to shift from your normal mode of communicating to theirs, accommodating their approach and "speaking their language."

Limits and Caveats

People have expressed concerns about using face reading to pre-judge and stereotype others. I would stress that as with any tool, it's only as benign and constructive as the person using it.

Face reading is not an answer to all things and certainly does not claim infallibility. The human psyche is far too complex to be pinned down to an all or nothing approach. Instead, one must understand that the traits on a face indicate interactive parts of the person's mode of expression. The two focal words are "interactive" and "parts." They show innate tendencies which can be read with an accuracy in the high ninety percent range, but should never be held as an absolute "it's on your face so it must be true."

Always remember that people, like all living things, are constantly growing and changing. Their approach can vary at any moment, change with the environment, and make subtle or major shifts over time. Life-changing experiences change us. Anyone can choose to suppress or overcome a given trait through directed will. We may find that our environment doesn't support certain parts of who we are and we change to meet the demands of our environment. We grow up and choose to harness certain traits rather than give them free rein. All of these can affect a reading because they can affect whether and how a trait is expressed.

Plus, never forget that traits interact. It takes a lot of files working together to make a scanner do what it does and it takes a lot of traits working together to make a person behave the way he/she does. No one trait tells the whole story and no one trait is unaffected by the others.

Face Reading as a Tool

There are many ways to learn about others. Face reading is a means to that end, a tool to make us more effective with less effort and time. It's a way to quickly assess personality traits and thereby understand and even predict typical behaviors. My intent is to provide the tool.

What I hope to do in this book is to broaden and deepen how you see people, and provide you with some sense of what is possible through reading the face and body. I want you to see how it can open windows into the whys of your own approach, turn on lights in the dark corners of other's behaviors, and give you a road map into the wilderness of communicating with those maddening fellow human beings on this bumpy highway of life. It's a gift of the possible.

If you're game to open this gift, read on.

Part I
ABOUT FACES AND IDENTITY

Badger

You have been reading faces all of your life and have probably never really thought about it. The body is an exquisite, living symbol of the person within and we instinctively grasp that symbolism, responding to different faces with different emotional reactions. But how and why?

Science has proven that everything is energy, so we too, are energy that is vibrating at a slow enough speed to be solid. What is this energy that is vibrating? Discussing what has been theorized and what has been proven is beyond the scope of this book, but let's just say for the sake of simplicity that who you are inside shows outside, and the energy is that of our unconscious thought patterns. In other words, our inborn, unconscious thought patterns manifest as symbols of who we are. Liz Greene said it beautifully in her book *Relating:*

"When we look at each other's faces, we see there the symbols of inherent character traits. We express this instinctually in our talk of weak chins and determined jaws, scholarly foreheads and predatory noses . . . We are putting into words our unconscious perception that the body itself may be a symbol of the individual, and we see in physical form a crystallized, concretised distillation of the other standing before us."[2]

As everyone knows, we are each the product of a long line of genetic material and those DNA codes have a lot to do with not only how we look, what diseases we might develop, and when we physically mature, but also how we are predisposed to think, act, and be.

I believe attitudes, ways of perceiving, and unconscious thought patterns, as well as inherent abilities are passed along in the DNA. They are "bred in the bone" and reside in the bloodlines. The innate abilities and inclinations provide both the what and the how of experience. Who we are by nature has a lot to do with our choices of experience as well as how we will perceive and respond to those experiences.

Today's sociologists, psychologists, scientists, and philosophers have pretty much agreed that who we are is predicated by both nature and nurture, but they fight over the question of the percentages. One recent book by an MIT professor of psychology, Steven Pinker, claims that we give far too much credit to the environment and not nearly enough to the genes.[3] He suggests that quite a large proportion of who we are is not conditioned responses, but *a priori* nature. I tend to agree.

It's the old chicken-or-the-egg question: were you predisposed, or did experience predispose you? And the truth of the matter is, you can't separate them. You wouldn't have the same experiences or see them the same

2. Greene, Liz, *Relating*, Samuel Weiser, New York, 1977
3. Pinker, Steven, *The Blank Slate, The Modern Denial of Human Nature*, Viking, 2002

way without being who you are. Yet having the experiences has an effect on the way you see yourself and hence, the way you react to subsequent experiences. Otherwise, there would be no psychological growth, but so much of *how* you filter it is inborn and will seldom change.

As an example, were you born with a wide face? If so, you were very likely strong willed even as a child, unafraid to explore your surroundings or greet strangers, and went to meet the world with little anxiety. So you chose many of your experiences based on who you are (go to meet the the world) and you responded according to who you are (unafraid). On the other side of the coin, if you were born with a narrow face, you were probably a lot more timid about new things and people so you chose experiences differently and responded to them differently (with considerable anxiety and an indirect approach, or even downright avoidance).

Jessie

My son had a long, narrow face as a toddler, and when the neighbors came to visit, he would run to his room, crawl under the bed and refuse to come out. The little boy next door had a wide face and he would climb into your car if you didn't get out quickly enough. He tended to go after what he wanted, no holds barred.

Those are single-trait examples, and of course, no one is a single-trait person. Everything affects everything. And what we expect to see (our perceptive filters) will affect how we translate what we actually see or experience. The traits shown on a face are indicators of some of our filters, hence our expectations and our associated behaviors.

Our tendency is to view our world and experience it through certain innate parameters and expectations that will determine how we behave and assign meaning to everything that happens in our lives. In many respects we are hardwired in our responses, but I also believe that *when we understand our innate tendencies, then we are at choice to behave differently* and affect our world through changing from within. If that change is profound enough, the face will change to reflect it. *(See page 18.)*

I had a first-hand experience of this after I had been reading faces for several years. I came across a picture of myself taken in 1992 when I was

1992

still working in the print/publications business (top picture). In that field, it is necessary to have a keen eye for minute detail, noticing every tiny mistake. Look closely and you will see that my left eye slants downward. That is a naturally critical view, automatically spotting what's wrong with things. If you look further, you will notice I show no eyelids. These are probing eyes with a real need to know why and a tendency to question everything.

2002

In the current picture on the bottom (2002) you see both eyes are level and there are eyelids showing. I am no longer in the corporate world, managing publications and dealing with all the minute details of the printing technicalities on a daily basis, critically assessing everything. My eyes are level today, and I am less critical. I have more eyelids showing, so I'm more cut-to-the-chase rather than probing in my approach.

As people change, their faces can very well change to reflect what has become a new, habitual response. It doesn't always

9

happen, especially if the trait is simply suppressed rather than truly changed from within. I've had a number of people tell me "I used to do that, but I don't anymore." They have consciously chosen not to express that part of their nature. At some point, when it is so automatic that it is no longer conscious, the face will probably change to reflect it.

Look at photos taken years apart of people you know and notice the definite changes in the faces. After you learn what the traits mean, look again to see what inner changes have transpired. This is fascinating to research on your parents and grandparents.

Martin

The Importance
of Faces

Have you ever wondered why one of the most compelling images is that of the human face? Since man began painting and drawing pictures, one of the most commonly recurring themes is faces (except in cultures that have a religious taboo against it). Look around you today and notice how often faces are used on billboards, magazine covers, ads, famous paintings, sculpture, even decorative motifs.

Faces are such an unparalleled draw, that they are used to sell everything from magazines to medicines, from kitchen tools to ideas. Almost anything that is sold through advertising, advertisers will use or have used a face to sell it. Little else holds the same power of attraction, the same seductive fascination as a face, and especially a beautiful one.

Why faces? It's so automatic that the question seems ridiculous. Of course we like to look at faces. It's an innate, necessary part of our socialization. It is an instinctual response evoked from the moment we first draw breath and look to our mother's face for an answering set of eyes. It's a survival mechanism, and a point of inner connection, eye-to-eye; some say, soul-to-soul.

In our evolutionary development, the need for communal animals to recognize one another is crucial to social interaction and survival. In animals, recognition of each other is primarily a function of scent. In humans it is largely a visual pattern recognition and a function of the cerebral cortex, the thinking part of the brain. Evolution has devoted a surprisingly large proportion of the human brain exclusively to facial pattern recognition.[4] That's why we can recognize people quickly and easily, even after seeing them only one time.

We all recognize a symbolic face: two eyes, nose, and mouth. The key to individual recognition is proportional differences. The pioneering work of Susan E. Brennan of Stanford University showed that people recognize a caricature faster than a realistic drawing.[5] A caricature is an exaggeration *of the proportions*, which translates to an enhancement of the pattern.

Those same proportions are what indicate the traits in face reading. So learning to read faces is comparatively easy because it is learning to discern relative sizes and proportions — determining what constitutes a wide space between the eyes, what shows high eyebrows, how high the forehead is relative to what, and so on. Then you commit to memory what each feature means in terms of innate need, response, or attitude, and the resulting behaviors. It's like learning a language. You learn the parts of speech then you put them together into sentences and paragraphs so you express an idea and understand more than the words. You read a face in the same way: as an expression of being, or the idea of a certain "you."

> **How Unique Are You?**
>
> Some lotto games use 6 numbers out of 54 and the odds of your choosing those same 6 numbers correctly is one in 25,827,165. People have many more personality elements than a mere six. I typically spot-read about twenty-two traits. What are the odds that another person would have exactly the same twenty-two elements in the same combinations and in the same degree as you do?

4.. Landau, Terry, *About Faces*, Anchor Books, New York, 1989

5. Brennen, Susan E., "Caricature Generator: The Dynamic Exaggeration of Faces by Computer," *Leonardo*, Vol 18, no. e, pp 170-78, 1985

The Uniqueness of a Face

We know that no two faces are exactly alike and no two people are exactly alike. Most people know that even "identical" twins are not identical. There are subtle differences that a careful study will discern and there are also matching subtle differences in their behaviors. I read a pair of twins at a party recently. The two women sat down together and pointed out the obvious: "We are identical twins."

"I see that, but you do know you are not identical, don't you?" I asked.

They laughed. "We know that but most people don't. I'm surprised you can see it so quickly."

"I love to draw people and have been studying minute details of faces most of my life. Learning face reading has just upped the ante," I explained. As I read their faces, I pointed out the likenesses and differences that showed and what each meant in terms of the differences in their behaviors and approaches. The variances showed in small proportional discrepancies and translated to personality nuances that affected behaviors. Both agreed with my analyzes of their subtle dissimilarities.

To reiterate, no two people are exactly alike and you begin to understand that on a profound level when you delve deeply into the world of reading faces.

The Mystery of Personal Identity

The human face is a wondrous creation. The structural details of its form holds some of the keys to the mystery of personal identity. In most societies, how we look is an innate part of how we think of and see ourselves in relation to the outside world. And of course, how we look is the primary factor in being recognized by others.

13

Consider for a moment, that if you looked totally different, would you *be* totally different? The answer is an unqualified yes. When people undergo a complete makeover; hair, makeup, clothes, they often rush home and slip back into the familiar style as much as possible. Why? "It's not who I am,"they say. The more drastic the makeover, the harder it seems to be to integrate into one's self image.

How we look has a profound effect on our sense of ourselves. We dress and groom in accordance with an internal image we hold of who we are. Where does this self-image originate? Part of it is from ways we've learned to perceive ourselves through our interactions with others, beginning with our earliest caregivers. Part of it is that underlying sense of a separate "me" that we identify with when we look in a mirror. But I believe the strongest aspect of personal identity is how we have approached the world from the very beginning, through the innate temperament we were born with. Any parent can tell you, a baby is not a blank slate, but each has its own personality from day one.

To help understand various facets of personal identity, many studies have been done on twins and several studies on identical twins who have been raised apart since birth. Researchers have found that those separated twins have many of the same approaches, tastes, quirks, and personality characteristics that are obviously innate to who they are and quite independent of their upbringing.

Psychiatrist Peter Nerbauer tells of one pair of identical twins who were separated at birth who were both anal retentive, quite unable to tolerate a messy environment. One said it was because his adoptive mother was a slob and it drove him crazy. The other said it was because his adoptive mother was very anal and he picked it up from her. As identical twins, they both had a number of traits on their faces which show they are predisposed to be extremely neat and clean *regardless of their upbringing.*[6]

Does Your Face Indicate Your Spirit?

Not really. For all that the face will tell about you, what the face won't tell is your inner being, for the soul of being doesn't reside in the structure of the face any more than the soul of the driver is determined by the kind of the car he drives. It will tell many things about your personality and how your will tend to behave while making this journey, but not who's within.

Face reading is a matter of understanding the personality, the outer expression of a person's being, but the spirit of the soul within can always choose to express differently to varying degrees. *(See Sample Reading, Mohandas Gandhi, page 150.)* It becomes a matter of awareness, conscious choice, and self-discipline to change our natural behaviors. Fortunately for the face reader, most people innately express from that automatic reaction space rather than from one of consciously choosing.

---

6. Wright, William, *Born That Way*, Knopf, 1998

Kurt

Part II
USING FACE
READING

Clarence

I believe life is an opportunity to grow, to experience, to understand, and through understanding, to gain wisdom and compassion.

Reading faces can be a part of this growth toward wisdom and compassion. When you understand your own traits and what they mean in terms of your own behaviors and attitudes, you begin to see what you have to work with in this life and grasp that it's up to you how you use it. The gift is you now realize you are at choice in your behaviors. Understanding your own traits can help change how you *choose* to operate. Knowing you respond automatically as an expression of your natural traits, you also know that you don't have to be limited to that expression unless you choose to be.

Now you are in a position to ask yourself a critical question about any behavioral characteristic, and that is, "does it serve me?"

If the answer is no, then you can begin to find ways to choose different behaviors, responding consciously instead of reacting automatically.

Let's say you have wide-set eyes, which means you tend to feel that situations are "out there" somewhere and not immediate, so you put off doing things until there is more pressure to get it done, like when it's due tomorrow! For example, if you are presenting a talk next week, you may wait until the day before the presentation to begin preparations. At that point you may realize there are more facets to this process than you realized and you don't have time to incorporate everything you really need. So you scramble and possibly do a mediocre job.

When you understand this is an aspect of one of your traits, you can catch yourself in the beginning stages of procrastination and choose to start early, pushing yourself to get completely involved while there is plenty of time to do the best job possible.

That's one small example of the possibilities open to anyone working with face reading. Another possibility is to understand *why* others naturally do what they do and find ways to work within the parameters of that knowledge, whether it is as a partner, parent, supervisor, counselor or friend. You have a broader perspective and truer expectations of others.

You realize their behaviors are legitimate, and impeccable to who they are. None are right. None are wrong. Some are better suited to one thing, others are better suited to another. Some traits serve us well, some don't. While certain aspects of traits can be problematic, no trait in and of itself is "good" or "bad." There are positive and negative expressions of each one. And who's to say, in the grand scheme of things, what serves another and what doesn't. All we're qualified to judge is what serves us and what doesn't, then respect another's right to choose for themselves.

When another person's behaviors causes us problems, then we certainly have a right to talk about how it affects us and work out a compromise. Generally speaking though, I believe it's better to work with our own traits and respect others' rights to be who they are.

17

In a nutshell, face reading helps you to accept yourself and others for exactly how we are, and then choose your responses appropriately. By so doing, it broadens the opportunity to make real choices and affect outcomes through understanding.

Face and Personality Changes

Science has shown that everything in the universe is basically energy vibrating at different speeds. Certain vibratory levels are slow enough that the energy is experienced as solid. Studies have found that each organ of the body has its own unique vibration and these have been mapped for use in the medical field.

So you could say that your body is simply energy that is given a particular form by the different combinations of vibrations. We could take that a step further and say that your own thought habits and beliefs are what hold your energy in it's own unique pattern, which is actually an integration of many vibrations.

Studies have shown that intense feelings of anger, hatred and related emotions are slower, lower vibrations than feelings of love and gratefulness. To me, this is suggestive that habitual thought patterns actually affect the physical configuration of the body through the vibratory levels.

I know that when you change an innate approach through conscious choice and/or life's demands on you, *and maintain that approach until it becomes habitual*, then your face can very well change to reflect the new behavioral style. For example, my son had a narrow face as a child and on into his twenties. Then he moved to Taos, New Mexico, and through a series of opportunities and choices, he wound up as the owner of four businesses with a broad clientele base, plus he became a regional director with the Search and Rescue volunteer operation. In the process, he grew quite confident of his ability to handle just about anything life threw at him. His face changed from a narrow one to a relatively wide face (without gaining weight), reflecting the comfort he has developed with facing new challenges. Metaphorically, you could say that inner self-trust expands one's being.

Enjoying Face Reading

Face Reading is a gift and a fabulously accessible one. If you work at it, you'll get to the point where you enjoy the insights that face reading can bring you about yourself and everyone around you. I encourage you to work (play?) with it. Do you want to understand relationships better? Try watching people to consider who might be most interesting due to their personality elements, or who would be most compatible with your own, or who might present a real challenge for you and why. It's great practice.

Or you can play with it as an innovative friend of mine did after taking a class. Being single, she noticed a nice-looking man at the next table wore no wedding band and he was dining alone, so she turned to her two female companions and told them, "I'm going to try out my face reading on that guy over there." They laughed, appreciating her chutzpa, as she got up and walked around to his table.

"Excuse me," she said, "I just took a class in face reading and I've been studying people. You have such an interesting face, I was wondering if you would mind if I practice by reading yours?"

He was surprised, but indulged her. She sat down and cautioned him that she was just a novice, but there were several things she could tell him. So, she read him, and asked for feedback. He smiled, told her the assessments were accurate and thanked her.

I'd like to say it was the beginning of a lifelong love affair, but alas, it was but a quick face reading. . . and a great story. The best part of it is that she saw enough in his face to know that he would be a good match on several personality traits and realized what a valuable tool it is in her quest to find a suitable life mate. She has been using it in all her first dates since — it makes her more fun and gives her valuable insights.

And that is what it's all about.

I never forget a face, but in your case, I'll make an exception.

— *Groucho Marx*

Grace

Part III
HOW DO YOU READ A FACE?

When I gave a talk at a nursing home, a woman raised her hand at the end of the presentation to ask how one goes about reading a face.

"What are you going to do, read my wrinkles?" she asked with a twinkle in her eyes.

"No . . . " I said as a preliminary to my answer.

"Good," she interrupted, "otherwise, we'd be here all day!"

Like that delightful character, people frequently ask, "How do you read a face?" That's a good question and I understand the need to ask it, because not too many years ago, I first heard the term "face reading" and dismissed the idea immediately. I could not imagine how you would "read a face," so I raised my hand in the classic gesture of "don't even go there" and walked away. I had to be talked into looking at it (and the rest, as they say, is history.)

So how do you read a face?

Before you can begin learning the trait elements, you need to know a few points about what the elements are, how you gauge them, and what to do with the information once you have it.

Point One: Trait elements are pieces of a puzzle

No one is simple and no one personality trait tells all. We are each a complex intermix of many trait elements.

So face reading is like learning a language: you have to learn the words before you can make sentences to communicate an idea. In face reading, you have to learn the personality elements or traits, then you begin to put them together to read a gestalt of the personality.

The traits in face reading are physical, outer indications of inner processes. Another way of saying it is that the outer form is created by the push of the inner function. Everyone has a chin, but the inner needs of a proportionally large chin will express a certain aspect of personality differently from the inner needs of a small chin. Which leads us to point two.

Point Two: traits are indicated by proportions and shapes

Personality traits are proportional and are on a continuum, from the high end to the low end. Remember what I said about patterns and caricatures — a caricature is an exaggeration of proportions.

That's how the elements work. The stronger the exaggeration of a given feature, the stronger that element of personality. The diagram on the next page shows how you begin to gauge the trait elements: high end, low end, and the middle ground.

Eyebrow Height

Selective   Casual

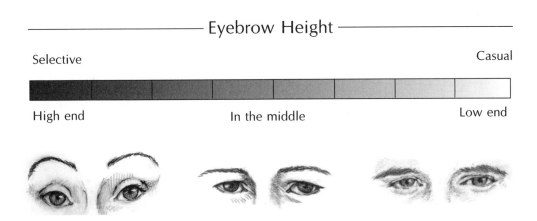

High end   In the middle   Low end

In this trait element, what you're looking at is the height of the eyebrows above the eyes. Each end indicates a different approach. The person at the high end does *not* understand the approach of the person on the low end and vice versa. They are worlds apart.

In the middle isn't really a particular expression like the two ends are. The person in the middle embraces both behaviors and doesn't exhibit the extremes of either end. They are more balanced in the expression of that trait element.

For example, on the left, the Selective person is very picky and standoffish. They exclude to feel safe. On the right or opposite end, the Casual person will tend to be more open to new people, may stand too close, and be too friendly. They include to feel safe.

The person in the middle will be reasonably friendly and stand a socially acceptable distance from others. Whether to be exclusive or accepting is not an issue for them the way it is for people at either end.

Point Three: Trait elements interact

Trait elements are small pieces of personality so no single one stands alone. The behaviors you would typically see with any given element can be enhanced or diminished depending on what else is present on the face (and in the psyche).

Let's take a pair of eyebrows and add two elements. Let's say someone who has high eyebrows (selective) also has small irises and her eyebrows are very straight, which can look like the woman to the right.

We'll call her "Veronica." She is even more standoffish than just selective alone would be, because those small irises tell us she doesn't like to show her feelings. She prefers to be an observer, taking an impersonal approach.

The eyebrows are straight, which gives her an additional reserve and an appreciation for the world of beauty and harmonious balance. In fact, she needs control and as little change as possible so her surroundings feel peaceful and predictable. Otherwise, she will want to escape the situation however she can manage it within the parameters of her world view. She will take a minimalist approach to expression.

You can see how both these additional trait elements enhance the selective, standoffishness, making it stronger.

Now, let's take the same eyebrow height and angle them upward into a dramatic upsweep, and give her very large irises, which you see below.

Let's call this one "Monique." Here you have a discriminating drama queen who wants the best and will definitely choose who she lets get close to her (selective). But — she also thrives on the theatrics of life, and loves to create an effect (upswept eyebrows).

In addition, she is very emotionally responsive (large irises) and hence her heart tends to rule her head. She generally can't keep her feelings under wraps and doesn't really see why she should.

These two additional elements diminish the highbrow standoffishness. But those high eyebrows will help her avoid getting too carried away emotionally without bringing some real selectivity into the process.

What you will likely see with this mix is still a discriminating person, but who will express herself for a maximum effect with a liveliness that's missing in Veronica.

Can you imagine how differently these two women might choose to dress and talk?

Point Four: Dominant features are dominant elements

Look for the most dominant feature or features on a face. They provide a good starting point, because they indicate the strongest personality elements. For example, the two faces below would give you two very different places to begin.

The man on the left is extremely mental in his approach (huge forehead), while the man on the right is very physical (large lower face).

People who are in the middle on most traits are harder to read, but they are actually more balanced. They *might* also be somewhat mild mannered, possibly wishy-washy. They could be very attractive as well, because studies have shown that what is universally seen as beautiful in the human face are average proportions, rather than exaggerated.

Be sure to keep these four points in mind when beginning to read faces: traits are pieces of a larger picture, they interact, you must gauge them on a continuum, and always be aware of what's dominant. When you do these automatically, you are well on your way.

Sofia

Part IV
BODY AND
FACE TYPES

Body shapes and face types can give you more information and enhance a reading. It can also help you quickly size up a new acquaintance before you study the details of the face.

First, we'll look at William Sheldon's three body types along with the basic temperament of each, then we'll look at body proportions and face types.

Three basic body types were identified by psychologist, William H. Sheldon in the first half of the last century. He developed a way to describe people in terms of physique and temperament and called them somatotypes.[7] He named them Endomorph, Mesomorph and Ectomorph.

People are a combination of all three body types. Some people have a strong dominance of one and they are the most easily typed. Others may have a dominance of two types and will exhibit a blend of the bodies and temperaments of both. The rest are more difficult to classify and it is pointless to attempt it here. In that case, turn to the face for information.

7. Sheldon, William H., *Varieties of Human Physique*, Harper Bros., 1940

Endomorph

The Endomorphic body type is naturally rotund, with very little bone or muscle definition. The bulk of their weight is in the gut, with a small chest and shoulders. Their extremities get shorter the farther they are from the body center, so they tend to have short arms but with longer legs and a high waist. Upper arms and thighs are large and ham-like. Hands and feet are usually small on this type, with short fingers and toes. They tend to get rounder with age.

Endomorphs are centered in the solar plexus region and operate from a "gut feel" about things. In fact, their gut is very important to them: they love to eat, digest, and socialize. The polite ceremony of family dinners are dear to their hearts, and they revel in the relaxed, slow-paced social graces. Groups stimulate them, fulfilling their craving for affection and acceptance. Isolation and social disapproval are utterly unbearable to them, and they will go to great lengths to avoid either, hence conventional values find a natural home with this group and that ensures the social acceptance and inclusion which is so important to them.

Endos readily express their emotions without inhibition, responding to others' feelings directly and sympathetically. The nurturing instincts are highly developed and easily invoked in this body type. When drinking, they become jovial, more relaxed and expansive.

Endomorphs sleep deeply and easily, sprawled out and snoring. Like other full-bodied creatures, Endomorphs move in an unhurried, almost indolent pace, their actions deliberate and slow, fully savoring all the sensory stimuli. Everything about them seems to run at a slower pace: their reactions, pulse rate, breathing, metabolism and speech. Even their body temperature and voices are lower than average. Because of this slowing down, Endos are prone to weight gain and circulatory ailments.

Major physical and temperament characteristics are:

- Skin is soft and apple smooth
- Fine skin, spherical head with round, broad face
- Tendency to fatness; rounded body with short limbs, high waist
- No bone or muscle definition
- Premature baldness beginning at the back top of head
- Relaxed, love of physical comforts and food
- Need acceptance, affection, and approval
- Love company, sharing meals, are excellent hosts
- Lower energy level, slow moving, slow reactions
- Relationship oriented, people loving
- Communicate feelings easily, are sympathetic
- Socially adept, generous to guests
- Complacent and tolerant
- Find isolation and social disapproval unbearable
- Deep sleepers, tend to sprawl and snore
- Conventional values
- Become jovial and expansive when drinking
- Nurturing, love children and babies
- Seek out other people when upset

Mesomorph

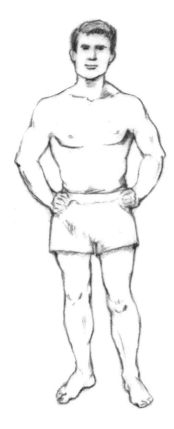

The Mesomorph body type has naturally well-defined musculature whether they are physically fit or not. They don't have to work at it to appear to be in good physical condition. Their bone and muscle mass is heavy with a large upper body and long waist tapering to small hips.

The head tends to be large and rather cubic in shape, showing prominent cheek bones, a long, broad face and a heavy, square jaw. On the Meso men, the shoulder muscles slope down in a pyramid shape and the limbs tend to be very well developed and carried on a massive bone structure, which is obvious in the thick wrists, ankles and fingers.

Typically a Mesomorph will have coarse, "orange peel" skin that holds a tan well and tends to develop deep wrinkles, often making them appear older than their age. Sporting coarse, thick hair, it typically balds as a receding hairline.

Women who are strongly Meso will show a great deal of angularity and muscular definition, but will have finer skin and hair than their male counterparts. However, they too will have a strong upper body with heavier bone and muscle mass than other women. They will hold a tan well, wrinkle more deeply and age more quickly. You will also see more warmth, cheerfulness, and socially acceptable behaviors than their male counterparts. Male and female Mesos are uninhibited about pursuing whatever they want, often riding roughshod over obstacles and people. Action oriented, they have high energy and good stamina and along with a hot temper and argumentativeness. They will often try to intimidate rather than reason or compromise. Social graces are not their forte. They are noisy, have resonant voices, eat rapidly without ceremony, and when drinking they are likely to become aggressive and very physical.

Success and status oriented, they are proud and self-centered, and if they aren't told often enough how wonderful or good-looking they are, they will state it themselves. Identifying characteristics are:

- Physically strong body, coarse skin and hair
- Massiveness in skeletal system, very muscular
- Natural athleticism, competitive, aggressive
- Only respect strength and courage
- Love physical adventure, risk, gambling
- Great need for recognition, status, and strokes
- Bold and direct, goal oriented
- High energy, assertive, ruthless, enjoy power
- Strong voice, noisy in general, don't care what people think
- Thrashing, noisy sleepers, need less sleep than most
- Indifferent to pain, heat, cold, noise
- Mature early, appear older than their age
- Not in tune with inner self, dreamworld or others' feelings
- High blood pressure and large blood vessels
- Hot tempered, argumentative, prone to physical acting out
- Need lots of space and freedom
- Uninhibited about nudity, warm up sexually very quickly
- Take physical action when upset

Ectomorph

The Ecto body type is thin and delicate with an overall look of elongation. The physical build is decidedly narrow with long legs, arms, hands, and neck, topped by a triangular face with a receding, pointed chin. The bones are small and delicate, thighs and upper arms thin and weak. In a sense, Ectos are more exposed to the environment, lacking either body fat or an armor of muscle to protect them and a nervous system that is more tightly hardwired than other types, so they register a physical shock reaction to sudden loud noises.

Typically an Ectomorph has unruly hair that is very fast growing and seldom balds. In fact, they tend toward hairiness overall.

Ectomorphs are often hunched over at the shoulders like an Ichabod Crane, partly because they hold a lot of tension in their shoulders and partly because they are basically shy and timid. Along with this shyness is a general quietness; soft voices, a light step, and light, fitful sleepers who sleep on their sides with their knees drawn up. Their worst nightmare is being subjected to a lot of noise or noisy people. They tend to be loners, can feel alone in a roomful of people, and prefer to observe rather than interact.

Motivated by a need for security (emotional, financial and intellectual), they are slow to commit, but very loyal once they feel secure with someone. To feel emotionally secure with a lover, they must be reassured often that they are the "one and only."

Unlike the other body types, Ectos don't operate from a center: it's as if they have antennae absorbing everything around them with no screening filter. Because they are so "out there" in sensory terms, they are introverted emotionally, needing privacy and a lot of time alone.

Typical behaviors and physical characteristics include:

- Slight, narrow build, small bones
- May have dry, almost scaly skin that burns easily and does not hold a tan
- Focus is on restraint, voice is soft, doesn't project
- Extreme sensitivity to pain
- Chronic fatigue, poor sleepers who suffer from insomnia
- Intense, apprehensive, with an otherworld quality
- Need protection from excessive stimulation with time to process experience — alone
- Hypersensitive, with instantaneous physical reactions
- Roving mind, impatient with slow pace of social chit-chat
- Avoid drugs, alcohol; fight anaesthesia and hypnosis
- Use indirect means to an end; not confrontational
- Very self aware, reluctant to show feelings outwardly
- Blood pressure is below normal, pulse is weak and fast
- Respiration is shallow and rapid
- Tend to eat small snacks, can't handle big meals
- Nervous stomach and bowels
- Late maturing physically, seem younger than their age
- Tightness in movement, posture; intertwine legs and arms
- When upset, will withdraw, hide out

Body Proportions

Gauging the general body proportions can be another clue to certain behaviors and physical needs. In this case, the proportional ratio between the torso and the leg length is the indicator.

Short-legged

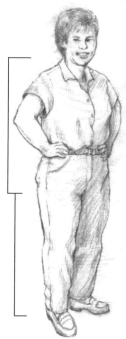

A person with short legs and a long torso is loaded with a lot of physical energy and a great need to be moving, so much so that it is difficult for them to sit still even when they are tired. If they aren't sleeping or physically incapacitated, they will be in motion.

The fact is, they do their best thinking while on their feet because they are kinesthetically oriented. When working through a problem, they will typically pace or do something mindless that allows them to process via activity and physical movement. Children with these proportions learn best through physical activities and a hands-on approach rather than seated at a desk.

If you are dealing with someone who is short-legged, be mindful of their need for movement. Desk jobs are especially hard on these people and so is asking them to sit still for meetings, discussions, or long dinners. They make good delivery people, liaison workers, sales people, waiters, coaches, construction workers, or anything else that requires being on their feet most of the time. Company presidents with this build typically spend much of their time managing from the floor rather than from behind a desk. Of course this physical drive depends on what other traits a person has, as well as their general health. I've read a couple of short legged people that tell me they are basically couch potatoes. There are exceptions.

I have found that a nearly equal dominance of Endo/Meso gives a disproportionately large upper body, small hips, short legs and incredible strength, drive and stamina. They are human dynamos.

Long-legged

The long-legged people really do have a need to sit frequently or they can easily develop back problems. Some people who have long legs and a lot of physical restlessness (large chin area, coarse skin and hair) get caught in the cross-fire of their traits and typically develop problems with their back, knees and/or hips.

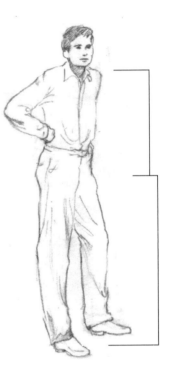

Long-legged people are a bit slower moving and have less stamina than their short-legged counterparts, tending toward mental rather than physical action. They don't expend themselves with the total physical abandon like Mesos and short-legged people, but rather bring a lot of mental energy to whatever they do.

Desk jobs are very appropriate for long-legged people, working in such fields as artist, programmer, accountant, secretary, seamstress, manager, and so on. If you have long legs (rather than average to short), you probably have a hard time keeping up with your short-legged friends both in terms of stamina and quickness of movement. I have a short- legged friend who is the same height as I am and when we go places together, he hits the pavement with both legs pumping. He's halfway to the store by the time I get out of the car, and I'm not lethargic.

Face Types

Face shapes are another means of typing. You can look at the overall shape of a face and get an idea of a person's general approach before you get into the specifics of the traits on the face. It is a kind of gestalt of varying trait combinations that can be a shorthand to personality. While the element names have been taken from Chinese face reading, the meanings are based on Western traits in combination and the descriptor defines the underlying approach.

The first shape is the Fire Face, a diamond shape.

The forehead slopes inward and the jawline angles to a point, so the widest part of the face is at the cheekbones. The chin is square.

Characteristics are:

- Risk-taking, adventurous
- Impatient, hot-tempered
- Short attention span
- Stubborn, contentious
- Need respect
- Good in a crisis
- Physically courageous
- Intelligent, but not subtle
- Don't delegate, may overextend
- Fast-moving

Fire
(Warrior)

The Wood Face has a rectangular shape. The forehead is the same width as the jawline and is squared, and the chin is rather rounded. The cheeks are relatively flat.

Characteristics are:

- Cautious and guarded
- Future-oriented
- Reflective and deliberate
- Quietly assertive
- Have definite opinions
- Good leadership qualities
- Build slowly, carefully

The Water Face is very round. All the dominant lines of the face shape are rounded: round sides, round chin, round hairline. The widest portion is at the cheekbones or slightly below them.

Characteristics are:

- Relationship-oriented
- Nurturing
- Adapt to circumstances
- Succeed through relationships and political savvy; subtle
- Good hosts, may be good cooks
- Strong drive for success
- Energy is softer
- More lethargic, slower moving
- Can multi-task well

The Metal Face is basically a square. In the pure form, you will see a lot of bone structure that underlies the flesh of the face, giving it a hard look. The cheek bones are prominent, but not fleshy, the chin is squared and the hairline is also squarish.

Characteristics are:

- Strong and unbending
- Physically courageous
- Direct, deliberate, linear
- Thorough; future-oriented
- Natural leadership abilities
- Short-tempered and demanding
- Objective, impersonal
- Take charge automatically

Metal
(General)

The fifth face type is not so much determined by the shape as it is by the size of the features. The features are all large, definitive, heavy looking. There's nothing delicate or sharp about them. This is an Earth Face: it has weight!

Characteristics are:

- Stately, slow-moving
- Tough minded
- Enjoy the sensual world
- Like power, territorial
- "My way or the highway"
- Can be demanding
- Loyal to friends
- Discreet and proud
- Money and status are very important

Earth
(Boss)

Mix and Match

I have found that the various face types don't necessarily match up with the various body types in any consistent manner. Looking at the two gestalts (face type and body type) on a person will give you some intriguing information for a very quick read. Then if you have time, you can study them more closely for more specific information about the individual combinations of traits shown on the face.

The other thing to be aware of is that *many people won't fit neatly into any of these gestalts.* You will see parts and pieces of the various types. Sometimes you'll recognize a face type, but not a clear body type. Other times it may be the opposite. Or you may not identify either.

Overall, in exhaustive studies done over the years, the various personality typing systems have been found to accurately fit about 37 percent of the population. The rest will have varying degrees of fit (usually above 60 percent) but not a clean match. The same is probably true of the face and body types. Face types are based on a particular combination of traits. A person may have all of them or a predominance of them and fit many of the characteristics. Others will have a hodge-podge of traits that don't fit into a pre-determined combination.

The purpose of learning these types is so you can get a great quick read a little over a third of the time. Other times, there may be enough of two types that you get a sense of who they are quickly and intuitively.

Which brings us to the beauty of face reading: it doesn't attempt to fit you into a "type." Learning the face and body types along with the individual traits allows you to identify the uniqueness of each person and integrate all the bits of information into a cohesive whole. You reach a point where you can see conflicts within the person, as well as the strengths, weaknesses, and gifts.

Part V
THE TRAIT ELEMENTS

The trait elements are those small, individual parts of personality, rather like pieces of a puzzle that you read and slip into the whole layout of a person so a more complete picture emerges. Then what you are looking at is a combination of nature and nurture with the added bonus of understanding and predicting typical behavior patterns.

You find that it's no longer such a mystery as to why people act the way they do. As a face reader, you note the behavior, look at someone a bit more closely and say to yourself, "Oh, well, no wonder."

It's like the perennial flirt who kept asking me why I wouldn't go out with him. I finally glanced toward his hairline and said, "Sorry. I've seen that forehead before." He was so flabbergasted that he never asked again.

I've been asked, "Isn't that stereotyping or prejudging?"

No more than going out with a man who takes his sixth mixed drink of the evening and mentions several times about all the fun he's had while drinking. You could be excused for concluding he has a problem with alcohol and deciding not to pursue the relationship any further. It's not judging so much as paying attention to the clues and choosing.

In reading faces, you understand what it means when traits combine in ways that are not compatible with your own or that spell conflicts you may not care to visit, so you select what you want in your life. That's making informed decisions — which you would do anyway, but do it in a longer time frame by having to experience the traits in action, then piece together conclusions about the personality. Face reading is a shorthand version to the same probable conclusions.

Like anything else, face reading can be used any way you choose. How you use it is more a function of who you are than what it is. It is a tool and a tool in your hands becomes what? That is for each person to answer. I simply offer the tool and hope it will be used for greater understanding, better choices, better communication and perhaps even greater tolerance and compassion for the plight of all human beings. After all, no one is perfect.

How to Use This Material

Start with one trait pair and really learn it. Use it for a few weeks until it becomes second nature to notice where a person fits on the scale and what it means about them.

Then when that one is quite secure in your automatic response to people, learn another pair of traits and use both pairs in your scan routine. After you feel solid about both sets of them, then begin noticing the combinations of the two and how the different combinations give you different behaviors. (Refer back to pages 24 and 25 to see how to do this.)

If you take this slowly, building your repertoire of knowledge and practicing daily, you will become adept at understanding what you see.

Now, let's look at the personality elements themselves.

COARSE SKIN & HAIR
"Tough"

Motto: "Bring it on!"

Gene enjoyed the outdoors regardless of the weather. He saw no reason not to hike and jog in 110° heat or below zero cold and slept with a window open, whatever the temperature. His wife, Candi, suffered through it for several years before finally declaring she would sleep in the next room when the weather was extreme. At first Gene was furious, but finally realized she was actually miserable from the effort to be with him and agreed to close windows when she asked.

"You're just a delicate little flower," he teased her.

"Baloney. If I were delicate, I'd be dead by now!" she retorted.

Always remember that the expression of a trait depends on what other traits a person has, their inner being, and experience. The following is a description of a "pure" expression of this trait without regard for other factors.

Internal toughness, relatively invulnerable to environmental extremes: heat, cold, noise.

Coarse skin and hair shows an internal toughness, an invulnerability to the environment. They can tolerate far greater extremes without feeling overwhelmed by them. In fact they enjoy strong stimulation like heavy, spicy food and primary colors. A Tough person can seem larger than life, reveling in the physical world. If they like it, more is better and even if they don't, it takes a lot to get under their skin. Heat and cold, coarseness, dirt, and strong odors don't bother them.

Tough people take difficult situations in stride and push through to solutions. You also find that they "let it all hang out," and seldom care what other people think. They are going to do what they like and if someone doesn't like it, it's not *their* problem. Subtleties and nuances often don't fully register with these people. It's not their focus.

Conditions most of us would consider extreme are seen by Tough people as minor inconveniences. To them it's unacceptable molly-coddling to refuse to work under such conditions and they figure you just have to rise above the situation. Obstacles are mere nuisances that they bulldoze through.

To their credit, they don't expect any more of you than they do of themselves, and "if I can do it, there's no reason why you can't." Sounds reasonable enough, but they don't realize it takes another Tough person to do it.

Physical Indicators
- Skin is very coarse: pores are large, creases in skin deep and pronounced
- Hair is coarse, sometimes curly or kinky.

Behavioral Characteristics
- Loud voice and laugh
- Authentic to self regardless of others' opinions
- Insensitive
- Vigorously active
- Like strong flavors, loud music, bright colors
- Unstoppable
- Direct, hot tempered

Famous People with This Trait:
- Margaret Thatcher
- Golda Meir
- Nelson Mandela
- Harrison Ford

Enhanced by
- Large chin, Metal face
- Low eyebrows
- Wide forehead
- Good muscle tone

Diminished by
- High eyebrows
- Narrow forehead
- Poor muscle tone
- Water face

43

FINE SKIN & HAIR

"Sensitive"

Motto: "Quality and moderation."

Marilyn felt beautiful and appreciated. Greg's fine taste was such a breath of fresh air after that disastrous first marriage. She had to wonder why she had ever married Darryl: he was uncouth in so many ways. His guns, camping, hunting, booming voice, rough hands — a Hemingway figure that was romantic to read about, but a horror to live with!

Greg came to the door, the absolute gentleman, clean hands, manicured nails, stylish clothes, and he smelled good. "You look stunning, Marilyn!"

She smiled in contentment as she took his arm. Her kind of man.

Always remember that the expression of a trait depends on what other traits a person has, their inner being, and experience. The following is a description of a "pure" expression of this trait without regard for other factors.

High degree of physical sensitivity with very little protection from the environment

Sensitive people are like hot-house flowers: they don't thrive in extreme conditions and with prolonged exposure can become overwhelmed. You know you are Sensitive if you have a very narrow setting on your comfort thermostat, quality is far more important to you than quantity, you are repulsed by loud, sweaty "he-men," can't sleep if the dogs down the block are barking, and your idea of camping out is a five-star hotel with all the amenities.

Sensitives have a delicate physical system and very little insulation to protect them against the environment. They need a moderate environment and a quiet space to live or at least to retreat to. When it's too noisy, it's like a friend of mine put it: "Noise feels like something beating on me and it drives me up the wall. I can't stand it."

Their system is finely tuned and it can get overwhelmed rather easily. Too much of anything is hard on them, including large meals, loud music, and brilliant colors.

When Sensitive people build some muscle, it functions like body armor, alleviating the extreme sensitivity and allowing them to participate in life more comfortably.

Physical Indicators

- Skin is porcelain, lines are very fine
- Hair is baby fine, flyaway and sometimes thin

Behavioral Characteristics

- Prefer quality to quantity
- Easily chilled or over-heated
- Prefer soft music or silence
- Noise gets to them very quickly
- Vulgarity, coarseness and sweatiness are offensive

Famous People with This Trait

- Gweneth Paltrow
- Mia Farrow
- Mariah Carey

Enhanced by

- High eyebrows
- Ecto/Endo body type
- Poor muscle tone
- Low ears

Diminished by

- Metal face
- Meso body type
- Hard muscle tone
- Low eyebrows
- High ears

WIDE FACE
"Adequate"

Motto: "I can do it."

"Just because I've never done it is no reason not to tackle it," Sarah said. *"I know I can do it, I just have to figure out how."*

"I have a book on the subject . . ."Jane volunteered.

"Thanks, but I'd never read it. I prefer to learn hands-on."

Always remember that the expression of a trait depends on what other traits a person has, their inner being, and experience. The following is a description of a "pure" expression of this trait without regard for other factors.

Degree of innate trust in one's own abilities; a feeling of adequacy.

The Adequate person basically feels equal to new situations and most challenges. They believe they can do things they've never tried before and tend to look for the reasons something will work rather than fear it won't. These people look for strength in others, and have little respect for timidity or weakness.

A high degree of Adequacy indicates people who will actively seek a challenge then walk away once they've mastered it. Occasionally, they bite off too much and fail, but it doesn't stop them. They very well might be in over their heads and quaking in their boots, but you'd never know it: they can bluff their way through with astounding brass, intimidation, creative fibbing, or whatever it takes. No one hates to admit failure more than an Adequate person and if they have a round forehead, they can sidestep like a dancer. They need the freedom to try new things and learn best hands-on. Don't give them a book as a learning tool — just point out what needs to happen and give them a little time and space. They'll figure it out.

They like to be around people who are unafraid to "go for the gold," and surround themselves with competent people who can keep up with them. Being "big picture" in their approach and naturally thorough, they can handle details but dislike them. With flared nostrils, they won't delegate.

Physical Indicator
- Forehead is wide in relation to the height of the face

Behavioral Characteristics
- Unafraid to tackle the new and unfamiliar
- Need a challenge
- Thorough, tough-minded
- Bored with the known
- Learn best hands-on
- May intimidate others

Famous People with This Trait
- Condaleezza Rice
- Oprah Winfrey
- Winston Churchill
- Dick Cheney
- Jim Carrey
- Robin Williams
- Hillary Clinton
- Rosie O'Donnell

Enhanced by
- Coarse skin and hair
- Metal face
- Meso body type
- Flared nostrils

Diminished by
- Endo or Ecto body type
- Narrow nose
- Receding chin

NARROW FOREHEAD
"Cautious"

Motto: "I'll try."

Jason was a nervous wreck for a week before his big presentation to the upper echelon staff. Afraid that they would ask questions he might not know the answers to, he researched, made volumes of notes and worried about all that could go wrong.

"What's the worst thing that could happen?" Mark asked.

"I could freeze and forget everything. What if they think it's stupid!"

"If that was the case, they wouldn't have asked to see your ideas. Relax."

"I can't until this is done. What if we lose power?"

Always remember that the expression of a trait depends on what other traits a person has, their inner being, and experience. The following is a description of a "pure" expression of this trait without regard for other factors.

Indicates a sense of inadequacy in the face of new and unfamiliar situations.

A narrow faced person will often come across as timid and fearful when confronted with a new situation. They feel unprepared for and unequal to these challenges and it seldom occurs to them to bluff their way through. Instead, they will try to postpone it if they've not had time to prepare.

Even when they have prepared, they generally feel some anxiety in confronting a new situation. Once they have succeeded, they become much more confident of their abilities in that area. The gift of these fears is a sensitivity to other people's concerns that Adequate people often lack.

The style most often displayed by a Cautious person is low key and indirect, perhaps even a bit pessimistic, focusing on the reasons why something could fail rather than why it could succeed. When they work with large projects, it's better for them to break it into smaller pieces to avoid the paralysis of feeling overwhelmed.

Because they are so aware of what they consider to be their own limitations, they often won't try things they feel are beyond their capabilities or knowledge. However, a few will drive themselves to early successes and develop beyond the typical limitations. These people can and often do rise to very high positions, but you will notice that they have a very different leadership style from that of their wide-faced counterparts.

Physical Indicator
- Forehead is narrow in relation to the height of the face

Behavioral Characteristics
- Cautious, somewhat timid
- More open to direction from others
- Willing to learn
- Prepare to avoid failure
- Often intimidated

Famous People with This Trait
- Meg Ryan
- Prince Charles
- Prince William
- Keanu Reeves
- Josh Groban
- Princess Diana

Enhanced by
- Fine skin and hair
- Wide set eyes
- Narrow nostrils
- Ecto body type
- Vertical forehead

Diminished by
- Coarse skin and hair
- Flared nostrils
- Meso body type
- Metal face
- Hard muscle tone
- Round forehead

49

HIGH EYEBROWS
"Selective"

Motto: "Only the best."

Patrice walked through three malls, checking all the stores in each, and at the end of the day came home with nothing.

"You found nothing acceptable?" William asked.

"Nothing," she replied. "I found very little of quality and taste, and even those were not exactly what I wanted. I'll find it eventually, but in the meantime, I'd rather do without than settle for something I don't really want."

Always remember that the expression of a trait depends on what other traits a person has, their inner being, and experience. The following is a description of a "pure" expression of this trait without regard for other factors.

Formal, aloof, and discriminating about who and what they allow into their world.

The person with high eyebrows will seem rather aloof and guarded, not easily accessible. They prefer to look a situation over before choosing to interact with people they don't know. Definitely not your typical warm and fuzzy hugger, always ask before touching them. It helps if you understand that they exclude for inner security, not snobbishness.

Being very particular in what they buy, where they go, what they eat, and who they socialize with, they usually have excellent taste and tend to be rather formal.

The kinds of comments you'll frequently hear from a Selective is, "But I don't *know* them," and "I wouldn't *have* that in my house." Theirs is a distaste for what they consider pedestrian values and objects. When they shop for an item, they are unwilling to settle for anything that doesn't truly meet their exacting standards.

Selective people are naturally protective of their emotional boundaries. They need time to assess your approach to life and to them before they decide whether they feel safe with you on an emotional level. This is just their natural way of being, so don't take it personally. They must have time to decide how they feel about things, people, new information. Don't rush them. If they finally do choose you, it's quite a compliment!

Physical Indicator
- Eyebrows are high above the eyes

Behavioral Characteristics
- Aloof and dignified
- Formal
- Extremely selective
- Slow to trust
- Maintain personal dignity and strong boundaries
- Exclude to feel safe
- Make total commitments
- Take time making decisions

Famous People with This Trait
- Connie Chung
- Diana Ross
- Michelle Pfeiffer
- Queen Elizabeth
- Al Gore
- Laurence Fishburne

Enhanced by
- Fine skin and hair
- Close-set eyes
- Low ears

Diminished by
- Coarse skin and hair
- High ears
- Wide set eyes

LOW EYEBROWS
"Casual"

Motto: "May as well be friendly."

Tom walked into the party and spoke to everyone he encountered, shaking hands, putting an arm around the shoulder, touching people on the arm to make a point, laughing frequently. He settled at a table with Lindsay, a woman he just met.

"I was watching you greet all your friends here. How do you know all these people?" Lindsay asked.

"I don't know anyone here. But I figure I might as well be friendly. I'll decide after a bit if I really like them or the situation. If I do, I'll stick around. If not," he shrugged with a wry smile, "then I'm out of here."

Always remember that the expression of a trait depends on what other traits a person has, their inner being, and experience. The following is a description of a "pure" expression of this trait without regard for other factors.

Place little store on formality. Naturally friendly and inclusive in who and what they allow into their world.

A person with low eyebrows will seem quite at ease and friendly to just about anyone when they first meet them. They tend to touch whatever or whoever they like: it's part of how they relate to their world. Don't assume the friendliness means anything more than their style of interacting. Buying habits reflect their non-choosiness, often buying whatever is at hand and will adequately do the job. For some Casuals, they even extend the lack of choosing to their close relationships, simply going along with whoever chooses them.

Phrases you often hear from these people are, "It's good enough," or "A good friend of mine," which often refers to someone they know only casually or perhaps recently met. They consider everyone they've met a "friend" unless they prove otherwise. In talking to people, they may move in too close for comfort, invading personal boundaries without realizing it.

Uncomfortable with formality and all the rules it entails, "low brows" have a need to be accepted as they are, and resist the idea of having to meet certain standards to be okay. Formality is artificial to them — expect them to poke a bit of fun at people who are formal. And that friendly demeanor can change suddenly if you seriously question their position on something. They can be inflexible.

Physical Indicator
- No space between eyes and eyebrows

Behavioral Characteristics
- Informal and friendly
- Accept good enough
- Like to touch
- Few boundaries
- Inclusive
- Inflexible when their position is questioned

Famous People with This Trait
- Ben Stiller
- Sting
- Anthony Hopkins
- George W. Bush
- Tom Cruise
- Elvis Presley
- George Clooney
- Janet Reno

Enhanced by
- Fine skin and hair
- Low ears

Diminished by
- Coarse skin and hair
- High ears

UPSWEPT EYEBROWS
"Expressive"

Motto: "Do it with flair!"

Alyssa talked with her whole body and could never just quietly tell a story: she presented a story with all the dramatic effects. She was telling the story at work about how she rescued a stray cat from her swimming pool.

"I leaned out to pick up the poor, struggling cat, but it was so scared it clawed at me. So finally I grabbed it by the scruff of the neck and swung around in one swift move and just threw it," she said demonstrating the maneuver, and threw herself straight into the chest of the Vice President who rounded the corner at that moment.

And that was another great story which was not lost . . .

Always remember that the expression of a trait depends on what other traits a person has, their inner being, and experience. The following is a description of a "pure" expression of this trait without regard for other factors.

Have an inborn drive to express themselves. Innate awareness of how to create an effect.

Expressive people usually keep life around them lively, creating an effect with their words, their hands, their stories and their artistry. Even if they are more reserved, or were rigorously trained not to be so expressive, they still have the innate ability. You may see it slip out in more subtle ways, such as a delicately artful arrangement of the items on a shelf or using body language and pauses for an effect.

One hallmark of an Expressive is using the whole body to tell a story, from the vocal intonations and facial expressions to timing and body stance. They seem to have a wider range of expressions than most and a need to give full play to them. For some, it's quite difficult for them to behave in a sedate, minimalistic style for long.

Expressives love an audience for their theatrics, but with or without one, they have an inner drive to express themselves dramatically, being naturally attuned to creating a desired effect. Having to tone it down or repress it can feel stifling to them, but its full expression may be overwhelming to others. Artists, actors, musicians, and writers often have these sweeping eyebrows. I've noticed some who hold a calm, stoic demeanor, yet even then they are creating the effect they want to project. Most will have an affinity for some facet of the arts.

Physical Indicator
- Eyebrows that sweep upward from the center

Behavioral Characteristics
- Talk with hands, like to demonstrate, not tell
- May over-dramatize themselves, love theater
- Can act a part, adaptable
- Adept at creating effects

Famous People with This Trait
- Ashley Judd
- Kristen Johnson
- Michael Keaton
- Jack Nicholsen
- Colin Powell
- Mike Tyson
- Salman Rushdie
- Dolly Parton

Enhanced by
- Wide face and coarse skin
- Set back ears
- Flared nostrils
- Protruding eyes/muzzle
- Large irises

Diminished by
- Receding muzzle
- Forward set ears
- Deep-set eyes
- Small irises and fine skin

STRAIGHT EYEBROWS
"Reserved"

Motto: "Balance and harmony."

Brendan's family seemed to thrive on constant arguments over everything and nothing. He brought his girlfriend home with him one afternoon to get some favorite CDs to listen to at the beach. As they walked through the den they could hear his brother and sister arguing over how to load the dishwasher. Jessica gave Brendan a quizzical look, with a sideways glance at the battle in the next room.

Brendan rolled his eyes and shook his head as they went upstairs. "I told you it's constant. That's why I'm not home anymore than I have to be, then I try to stay in my room with the headphones on to drown it out."

Always remember that the expression of a trait depends on what other traits a person has, their inner being, and experience. The following is a description of a "pure" expression of this trait without regard for other factors.

Deeply affected by sensory input. Need harmony, beauty and balance in their surroundings.

Reserved people have a heightened sensitivity to sensory input of all kinds and don't function well in extreme surroundings. Frequently they will do things to create a peaceful, natural environment where they can feel the tranquility of it. They rarely create a disturbance and usually operate on an even keel, doing everything with quiet restraint and temperance: speaking in a calm, moderate voice, their physical movements gentle and soothing.

In a group, they promote peace and harmony and get very stressed when there's in-fighting, even to the point of abandoning the group.

Beauty and harmony touch the soul of the Reserved person, and they respond deeply though their feelings. The trouble is, they can go so deeply into their responses to the pleasurable, sensory world that they get lost in it, refusing to face the unpleasant realities and blaming others for the problems. There is a tendency to try to escape chaotic situations any way possible, and may run away rather than face and solve problems.

Yet, with their wonderful sense of balance and harmony and a deeply felt response to beauty and the sensual world, you often find this trait on people in fashion and the arts. Under calm circumstances, they are soothing to have around.

Physical Indicator
- Eyebrows are straight and longer than the eye

Behavioral Characteristics
- Seek harmony
- May be peacemakers
- Reserved, balanced
- Voice is midrange and evenly modulated
- Don't function well in chaotic conditions
- Strong responses to sensory stimuli

Famous People with This Trait
- Ben Affleck
- Wynona Ryder
- Laurence Fishburne
- Matthew Perry

Enhanced by
- Fine skin and hair
- High eyebrows
- Low ears
- Ecto/Endo body type
- Poor muscle tone

Diminished by
- Coarse skin and hair
- Meso body type
- Good muscle tone
- High ears

ROUND EYEBROWS

"Systematic"

Motto: "I like a system."

"Doris, can you come over and help me make sense of this mess?" Lydia wailed to her best friend. She was moving and Doris walked in to find rooms full of half-packed boxes, books and papers strewn about, drawers emptied on the floor and no systematic approach to anything.

"Why don't we start with the guest room, putting only books in these boxes, knick-knacks in those, the wall decor can go in these bigger boxes and we'll pack the clothes after we go through them. Where's a marker so we can label everything?"

"I never thought of that. You make it seem so simple."

"It is," Doris smiled.

Always remember that the expression of a trait depends on what other traits a person has, their inner being, and experience. The following is a description of a "pure" expression of this trait without regard for other factors.

Ability to integrate all the disparate parts into a cohesive whole and have it work.

Systematic people can organize a function, plan an office filing system, set up an employee vacation calendar and any number of other jobs that require the ability to seamlessly mesh the parts of a whole. In the face of new situations, they intuit where to start, what to do in what order, and can manage the entire process easily.

Women who love to join and run clubs frequently have these eyebrows. They make the best officers and especially presidents!

Systematic people can get irritated with other people's messes — unless they happen to be professional organizers, like those that grace the Oprah show and make a living transforming those messes into smooth-running operations!

These people have an innate ability to understand how the parts need to come together for a workable whole. In the midst of chaotic conditions, they have the mental capacity to create or discover a path to order through a systematic organization of the various pieces.

You sometimes find these eyebrows on mechanics or mechanically oriented people. They understand the whole and its parts and how to take something apart and put it back together — and do it without leftover pieces.

Physical Indicators
- Perfectly rounded eyebrows (must be naturally so, not plucked to achieve the curve)

Behavioral Characteristics
- Natural organizational and/or mechanical ability
- Irritated with disorganization and messiness
- Understand systems
- Good event planners

Famous People with This Trait
- Naomi Campbell
- Osama bin Laden
- Hillary Clinton
- Thora Birch

Enhanced by
- Flared nostrils
- Fine skin and hair
- Close-set eyes
- High eyebrows
- Low ears

Diminished by
- Coarse skin and hair
- Wide-set eyes
- Low eyebrows
- High ears

CLOSE-SET EYES
"Diligent"

Motto: "Do it now and do it right."

Margo freely voiced her opinions to her staff so they soon knew exactly what to do, how to do it, and what not to do. Anytime a new person asked the best way to make points with Margo, they were told by the staff, "Be prompt, be bright, and be gone."

Margo laughed when recounting this, then said quite earnestly, "And it's absolutely true. I will not allow people to waste my time."

Always remember that the expression of a trait depends on what other traits a person has, their inner being, and experience. The following is a description of a "pure" expression of this trait without regard for other factors.

Personal lens is set at micro focus: strong sense of immediacy and limited tolerance.

People with close-set eyes seem to operate in a pressure cooker. They have quick reactions, focus on what's right in front of them, and want everything done immediately and correctly. It's amazing how much work they can get done in a very short time. Like an air traffic controller they know what's lined up awaiting their attention, and what's in the air awaiting completion. They take care of one thing at a time, in order of priority, and keep things moving as efficiently as possible.

They have zero tolerance for procrastination and can be perfectionistic. Relaxing is out of the question until everything is complete, and for the Diligent, relaxing is a relative term — they relax by doing something fun. When they are finished with an interaction, they want you out of their space so they can move on to the next thing on their list.

In relationships, they can be demanding and high-maintenance without realizing it, partly because when they make emotional commitments, they are intense about them and partly because they perceive the world as black and white and react from that space, demanding that others meet their standards. They can also get upset over small issues and remain focused on the specifics, not the big picture. Generally, you'll find them extremely conscientious and dependable.

Physical Indicators
- Eyes are less than one eye's width apart

Behavioral Characteristics
- Don't waste time
- Specifics are important
- Can be nosy
- One thing at a time
- Abrupt when finished
- Intense, close focus
- Feel that matters are "in their face"
- Can't relax with things pending

Famous People with This Trait
- George W. Bush
- Sarah Jessica Parker
- Jennifer Aniston
- Barbara Streisand

Enhanced by
- Metal face
- Wide jaws
- Meso body type

Diminished by
- Endo body type

WIDE-SET EYES
"Lenient"

Motto: "It's not a big deal."

The neighbor's teenage son had a band and they practiced in the garage until midnight or later every Saturday night. The garage was next to Betty's bedroom. It was too loud to sleep most Saturday nights until they quit.

"Kids grow up and leave," she rationalized and figured that things will generally take care of themselves if left to percolate awhile. But after three months, the boys took it too far by opening the garage doors at two in the morning and cranking it up. Betty exploded."I've had it! This is going to stop NOW."

And it did.

Always remember that the expression of a trait depends on what other traits a person has, their inner being, and experience. The following is a description of a "pure" expression of this trait without regard for other factors.

Tends to be easy-going, put things off until the last minute, and take a big-picture view of life.

These people are very easy to be with. They see things in a broad perspective and take a philosophical approach to life and its vicissitudes. They don't get upset easily and will laugh off small irritations or simply set them aside as not worth getting bent out of shape about.

But don't take their good nature for granted. Yes, they've got a long rope, and yes, they can get to the end of it. And by the time they finally do, you've pushed them miles too far and you're likely to reap major repercussions. Be aware that when they've "had it," they may end the relationship.

To them, the world is somewhere "out there" toward the horizon and not in their faces. Their to-do list is rather fuzzy, with just a few things bobbing to the surface of their awareness, so they may procrastinate, miss deadlines or be late. And when they get involved in doing something, that's all they see and they can lose track of time entirely.

You might check in with these people occasionally to see if something bothers them, because they probably won't tell you until it's too late. Don't try to pin them down too tightly — this is an anathema to them. Give them a broad playing field, but set your own needed time frame, and specify why. Then loosen up around them. After all, they put up with quite a bit from you.

Physical Indicator

- Eyes are more than one eye's width apart — the wider they are, the stronger the trait

Behavioral Characteristics

- Accepting of situations
- Will procrastinate
- Easy-going
- Big picture approach
- Get involved and forget time
- When finally pushed too far, they explode

Famous People with This Trait:

- Britney Spears
- Oprah Winfrey
- Muhammad Ali
- Jackie Onassis
- Kevin Spacey

Enhanced by

- High ears
- Upturned eyes
- Coarse skin and hair

Diminished by

- Low ears
- Fine skin and hair
- High eyebrows
- Down-turned eyes

NO EYELIDS VISIBLE
"Probing"

Motto: " Why?"

Martin drove to five new car dealers in the Metroplex after he had read four new car magazines, three Consumer Report articles, and researched online for over a month. He wanted to check out the top cars by test driving them and questioning the sales people about the features and any known problems. When he finally drove home in his new car, it was with a feeling of completion and victory. He was satisfied it was the best choice.

" It's just a car," Randy needled him. "Why all the fuss?"

"Isn't making a good choice important to you?" Martin shot back.

Always remember that the expression of a trait depends on what other traits a person has, their inner being, and experience. The following is a description of a "pure" expression of this trait without regard for other factors.

Have an emotional need to make informed decisions based on all the facts and fit them into their particular world view.

A Probing person is seldom satisfied with just skimming the surface when they are expected to act on a subject; they have to know as much as possible about it. They are the original comparison shoppers and the "why babies." One of their passions is to figure things out and feel the rush of victory when they are right.

If you question or throw a new idea at them, they may sit and stare blankly as they process information, unable to accept any other input while they fit it into their framework. Don't misread it as stonewalling. What's happening is they are caught in mid-process and feel that any statement of position or a final answer is premature. They frequently answer a question with a question.

Tending to meander in their conversations, they like to cover all their bases plus everything remotely related that occurs to them before they finally get to the point in the last sentence.

Especially with a vertical forehead, these are "ducks in a row" people who don't function well until they have achieved mental order. They have been known to argue, interrogate, and push to have your viewpoint match theirs, because it doesn't make sense to them. After all, *they* have reasoned it all out and if you had too, you'd see it their way.

Physical Indicator
- No eyelids show with the eyes open normally

Behavioral Characteristics
- Analyze and compare options before committing
- Compulsion to know why and how
- Love to figure things out
- Can appear uncooperative while processing new information
- May enjoy mysteries and puzzles

Famous People with This Trait
- Leonardo di Caprio
- Brad Pitt
- Winston Churchill
- Faith Hill
- Sting
- J. K. Rowling

Enhanced by
- Vertical forehead
- Down-turned eyes and nose
- High forehead
- Wide-set eyes

Diminished by
- Close-set eyes
- Angled-back forehead
- Upturned eyes

LARGE EYELIDS
"Bottom Line"

Motto: " Cut to the chase."

Ellen sat in the meeting quietly until the third episode of "unnecessary information" derailed its timely conclusion. At that, she moved that the whole question be tabled until the people involved could work out the details in committee and bring back a solution.

"I have an appointment in ten minutes and we still have another question to vote on before we adjourn, so can we move on here?" she asked.

"It's a sensitive issue and people have a lot of feelings about it," Mary protested.

"I have a lot of feelings about it too, but at some point you have to set them aside and just get the job done. It's time to do that."

Always remember that the expression of a trait depends on what other traits a person has, their inner being, and experience. The following is a description of a "pure" expression of this trait without regard for other factors.

Indicates quickness of response to concepts and the need for immediate action.

A Bottom Line person can seem cold and unfeeling at times in their drive to get things done. Once they think they understand the concept, they act. Long explanations and all the related preliminary details are exasperating to them. It doesn't work to get into all the whys with a Bottom Line person: they really don't care. State the point first, then if you have to explain why, do it afterwards. But generally, unless they ask for reasons, don't bother.

Not people to get hung up in all the emotional baggage associated with life, they pride themselves on getting the job done regardless of how they feel. Even if a beloved dog of sixteen years just died, they will set the problem aside and go on to work because the job has to be done.

Relationships can be a challenge to these people because they tend to stuff their own feelings and expect their partner to do the same. They may get too impatient to hear them out, especially when something needs doing immediately.

"Cliff Notes people" at heart, it is difficult for them to sit and listen to all the details, but when they do, their gift is to take it in and summarize the key points immediately with uncanny accuracy.

Physical Indicator
- Eyelids are very full when the eyes are open

Behavioral Characteristics
- Like to "get on with it"
- Will ignore own feelings to get the job done
- Impatient with detail
- Cut to core issues
- Good with deadlines

Famous People with This Trait
- Susan Sarandon
- Anthony Hopkins
- Cher
- Julianne Moore
- Madeleine Albright
- Mother Theresa
- Michael Caine

Enhanced by
- Low eyebrows
- Angled back forehead
- Protruding muzzle
- Protruding eyes

Diminished by
- High/round eyebrows
- Vertical forehead
- Receding muzzle
- Deep-set eyes

LARGE IRISES
"Responsive"

Motto: "I feel what I feel."

Darla sat with her eyes brimming, watching a touching TV commercial while helping Danielle with her homework.

"Mom, are you crying about that commercial?" Danielle demanded.

"Are you ready for the next test question?" Darla dabbed her eyes as she talked.

"Why do you do that, Mom? You cry at everything."

"That's just the way your Mom is — she cries when she's happy, she cries when she's sad, she cries because she cries," John explained to their daughter.

Always remember that the expression of a trait depends on what other traits a person has, their inner being, and experience. The following is a description of a "pure" expression of this trait without regard for other factors.

Indicates a high degree of outward emotional responsiveness.

People with large irises will be overtly emotional and may cry at movies, when they are upset or angry, or even watching TV commercials. Expect them to talk on a very personal level, wanting to know about you and your private life. They come across as warm and friendly, enjoying the give and take of intimate relationships and are usually quite sentimental and able to listen sympathetically.

A Responsive person's decisions will be based more on how they feel about something than what they think about it, although they do respond to reason and logic. They often "think" with their hearts instead of their heads. Frequently this trait is present in charismatic people with their great enthusiasm and warmth.

If Responsive people seem to need more reassurance and approval than most, it's because they are more subject to guilt about their own actions in relationships, fearing they caused someone to disapprove or dislike them. They have a great need to be included and will tend to see everything you do as indicative of whether or not you like them. Eating with a Responsive person is like a bonding ritual to them and refusing an invitation is felt as rejection. They need to know that they are important to the people they care about, and indeed, that they matter, period.

Physical Indicator
- The irises are large, filling the eye

Behavioral Characteristics
- Very emotional
- Sentimental
- Tend to be warm and personable
- May cry easily
- Take things personally
- Need lots of attention and expressions of caring

Famous People with This Trait
- Katie Couric
- Laura Bush
- Sarah Jessica Parker
- Reba McIntire
- Salma Hayek
- Madonna
- Carol Burnett

Enhanced by
- Fine skin and hair
- Narrow face
- Protruding eyes
- Endo/Ecto body type

Diminished by
- Coarse skin and hair
- Wide face
- Deepset eyes
- Meso body type

SMALL IRISES
"Dispassionate"

Motto: "Stay cool."

There was nothing A.J. hated more than people overreacting, being sentimental, or prying into his personal feelings. When his boss, John, lost his temper and began yelling, it was all A.J. could do to stay in the same room with him. It was even worse when Gretchen tried to commiserate with him, and wound up crying in his car on the way to the staff meeting. He hated it.

"How was your day," Jessie asked when he walked in that evening.

A.J. took a deep breath. "Don't ask."

Always remember that the expression of a trait depends on what other traits a person has, their inner being, and experience. The following is a description of a "pure" expression of this trait without regard for other factors.

Indicates a low degree of outward emotional responsiveness.

A person with very small irises may seem cold, stoic, and quite impersonal. They seldom share their feelings because they are so deeply buried that emotional reactions are not immediate and obvious. In fact, they have an abhorrence of emotional exposure and display.

Dispassionate people are oriented toward keeping their cool and getting the job done. They are interested in efficiency and results, not in morale building and rah-rah approaches. Nothing turns them off faster. They may not actually be as tough as they seem, nor as cool inside, but the last thing they want to do is to blow their cover.

Usually, it's a good idea to stay on an impersonal basis with these people or at the least, a non-emotional basis. They find it insulting if you don't respect their privacy. It's humiliating to them to display any neediness or weakness and find overt efforts to commiserate with their problems an affront to their dignity. They don't brag and have little respect for people who do.

Oriented toward their own concerns, they are not nosy, and could even be called self-centered because empathetic connection requires emotional outreach and that is hard for them. In friendships, they can be funny and relatively friendly, but always with a bit of detachment and a definite personal boundary beyond which it's best not to push.

Physical Indicator
- Irises are small with lots of white showing.

Behavioral Characteristics
- Cool and reserved
- Dislike overt emotionalism
- Tend to have impersonal conversations
- Not "touchy-feely"

Famous People with This Trait
- Will Smith
- Kevin Spacey
- Colin Powell
- Hector Elizondo
- Rosie O'Donnell
- Naomi Campbell

Enhanced by
- Deep-set eyes
- High eyebrows
- Ecto or Meso body type

Diminished by
- Protruding eyes
- Endo body type
- Low eyebrows
- Full lips

EYES SLANT DOWN
"Meticulous"

Motto: "I notice inconsistencies."

Alice, still talking on the phone, took one quick glance at the ad and stabbed a finger in the middle of the central paragraph.

"Extra space there. The rest is fine." She handed it back to me and continued her conversation. I walked away dumfounded.

"Wow!" I exclaimed to a co-worker. "How did she do that so fast?"

"We call her Eagle Eyes. I've never seen her miss anything — and she's always that fast."

Always remember that the expression of a trait depends on what other traits a person has, their inner being, and experience. The following is a description of a "pure" expression of this trait without regard for other factors.

Shows the degree of evaluative perception. Able to critically evaluate things with ease.

A Meticulous person will seem nitpicky and very quick to notice the smallest errors, inconsistencies, and inherent flaws in everything from movies to misspelling and misaligned columns. They are hardwired to find what's wrong with things because their perceptive filter is set on ultra fine; it catches almost everything both right and wrong. They also notice the opportunities and possibilities that others often miss, understanding the specifics, not just generalities, and this is doubly so when the eyes are close together as well.

Good at evaluating projects, ideas, and works-in-progress, they can be a priceless resource. However, if you do hand something over to a Meticulous person, have it as perfect as as you can, then be appreciative of what they offer with their critiquing abilities. Expect laser-like details as to what could be better and what works as is, whether it's concept, design, or execution.

They have a strong sense of right and wrong with a natural emphasis on correcting the wrongs so when they find a problem, they want it fixed immediately. In a class, meeting, or presentation, they will be the ones who question everything closely, noticing any slight inconsistencies, probing for any other possible errors and wanting them corrected. . . publicly, now.

Physical Indicator
- Eyes slant downward, measuring from the inner corner to the outer corner

Behavioral Characteristics
- Notice problems
- Excellent at critiquing
- Spot inconsistencies
- Discover opportunities
- May be overly critical

Famous People with This Trait
- Carlos Santana
- Sarah Michelle Gellar
- Haley Joel Osment
- Helen Hunt

Enhanced by
- Close set eyes
- No eyelids
- Down-turned nose
- High eyebrows
- Low ears

Diminished by
- Wide-set eyes
- High ears
- Low eyebrows
- Upturned nose tip

UPTURNED EYES
"Overlooks"

Motto: "I didn't notice."

Marie bought a sweater she loved and decided to wear it the next day. That morning, she quickly snipped off the tags and pulled it over her head..

Taryn walked in, asked Marie to turn around for her to admire the new sweater, then said, "Did you know there is a small pull on the shoulder? You should take it back and exchange it, because otherwise, it looks great on you."

"Oh dear. Do you really think people will notice?"

Always remember that the expression of a trait depends on what other traits a person has, their inner being, and experience. The following is a description of a "pure" expression of this trait without regard for other factors.

Indicates a low degree of evaluative perception. May fail to notice problems and opportunities.

A person with upturned eyes is very easy to be around. They really don't notice problems and inconsistencies unless they are glaringly obvious. It's as if they see the world through soft-focus lenses that are quite forgiving of all the warts and chin hairs on everyone around them. The unfortunate thing is, it also doesn't register what's possible, unless that too, is quite obvious.

You could say their perceptive apparatus is set to such a wide grid that a lot slips through. People may accuse them of having their head in the clouds, so unattuned are they to the nitty-gritty details around them. Others may have to help them see details they tend to miss, or may need to probe a little and prompt them to focus in on inconsistencies and omissions that matter.

The upside is that they are so very not focused on problems that they may tackle their dreams without all the worries about possible obstacles and the attendant fears, and just work their way through them. They can also be so pleased with their own work that they never think to pick it to death. One woman I know who has upturned eyes happily put down her own tile and is delighted with it even though it doesn't quite meet at the edge in one spot and is uneven in height, but I suspect she hasn't even noticed!

Physical Indicator
- Eyes turn up from inner corner to outer corner.

Behavioral Characteristics
- Tend to miss flaws
- Not critical
- May be too optimistic
- Overlook details and opportunities

Famous People with This Trait
- Cher
- Salma Hayek
- Brandi
- Sandra Bullock
- Audrey Hepburn

Enhanced by
- Wide set eyes
- High ears
- Low eyebrows
- Coarse skin

Diminished by
- Close set eyes
- Vertical forehead
- Low ears
- Down-turned nose
- Fine skin

75

PROTRUDING EYES
"Enthusiasm"

Motto: "Be happy."

"I love Julie with all my heart, but I don't know if the relationship can survive. She is always wanting to get into blame, being sad and stuck in it. When I try to cheer her up, and tell her to just be happy, she gets mad at me, and I can't handle that." Brad told his best friend, Rosie.

"So what do you do when she gets mad at you?" Rosie asked.

"Go do something with someone who isn't into gloom and doom. Yesterday when she got mad again, I went to a Rotary fundraiser with Harry and Jack. I'm going to join their club. You should see the good things for the community; in fact, why don't you join, too!"

Always remember that the expression of a trait depends on what other traits a person has, their inner being, and experience. The following is a description of a "pure" expression of this trait without regard for other factors.

Indicates a tendency to embrace life with full participation and a positive attitude.

People often dismiss these cheerful Enthusiasts as inveterate Pollyannas, dripping with good cheer and hawking a pipedream of wishful thinking. They miss the point. Enthusiastic people instinctively trust that if you have a positive attitude and stay upbeat, good things will happen. Certainly folk wisdom supports their belief with sayings such as "You attract more flies with honey than vinegar," and "What you believe, you receive." Many authors and speakers have based books and careers on positive mental attitudes and it is espoused in thought as diverse as fundamental Christian televangelists and scientists who have found that the beliefs of the observer affects the outcome of experiments in particle theory. In essence: you get what you expect. "So why not expect good things in life," they ask. Good point.

However, there are three major challenges to this trait. First is dealing with the downside of life and people; the naysayers and cynics, the disasters that blindside us. These leave the Enthusiast feeling inadequate and angry. The second is overextending themselves through wanting to do all things with all people, all the time. The third is learning to allow others their privacy with observer status rather than participant. They have to learn it's okay to have light *and* dark, and to not always dance.

Physical Indicator
- Eyeballs appear to bulge in the sockets.

Behavioral Characteristics
- Love to participate
- Enthusiastically embrace whatever they do
- May push too hard for others to join them
- A need to be doing
- Shun experiences of grief and sadness, may berate people for having them

Famous People with This Trait
- Jim Nabors (Gomer Pyle)
- Susan Sarandan
- Goldie Hawn

Enhanced by
- Protruding muzzle
- Wide face
- Set back ears
- Angled forehead
- Low eyebrows

Diminished by
- Vertical forehead
- Narrow face
- Thin lips
- High eyebrows
- Fine skin and hair

DEEP-SET EYES

"Private"

Motto: "Stay out of my business."

The interview was moving along with a fine momentum until Michelle asked John about his personal life and how his early family experiences might have contributed to his unusual success as an engineer/architect. She didn't accept his lightly brushed over answers and began to probe.

" Your father was a high profile developer in the Midwest and stories of his excesses are legion. How would you characterize your relationship with him?"

"Like I said, it was fine."

Always remember that the expression of a trait depends on what other traits a person has, their inner being, and experience. The following is a description of a "pure" expression of this trait without regard for other factors.

Indicates a more inward approach to life that is both private and serious.

To the Private person, the business of living is a serious endeavor which they respect and treat as such. As they ponder each of the daily challenges to their space and time, they evaluate its capacity to harm or empower them before they choose whether to involve themselves. They are basically fortified within their own being, looking for what and who they can trust. For anyone to probe, question, or push them for what they have not volunteered registers as an invasion and is likely to be treated as such. It is akin to someone barging into their house and shamelessly digging into drawers and closets. It elicits a masked outrage response.

Private people will typically respect your privacy with the same ardor they protect their own. Because their feelings are private, you will seldom see them displayed. Even if they are furious, ecstatic, or terrified, the demeanor tends to be stoic and unrevealing. When you've overstepped the boundaries, you're likely to evoke some cutting remarks or an intense, impenetrable look, but don't expect to "talk this out." That's the last thing they want. What they *do* want is for you to back off. They have to learn to reveal themselves and it is never easy.

To their credit, if they truly commit to something, they will do it to the absolute best of their ability, taking the responsibility very seriously.

Physical Indicator
- Eyes are set back deeply under the suborbital ridge

Behavioral Characteristics
- Intensely private
- Serious
- Stoic demeanor
- Sarcastic when feeling invaded

Famous People with This Trait
- Tom Cruise
- Clint Eastwood
- George W. Bush
- John Travolta

Enhanced by
- Down-turned nose
- Small irises
- Pointed chin or wedge jaw
- Thin lips and small mouth
- Narrow or metal face
- Straight or arched nose

Diminished by
- Large irises
- Full lips, large mouth
- Round face
- Protruding muzzle
- High ears
- Scoop nose
- Endo body type
- Coarse skin and hair

ANGLED FOREHEAD
"Assumptive"

Motto: "Let's go."

J. B. would slip into action with a fine disregard for planning. His family learned early that you didn't ask questions and didn't get in his way if you valued your dignity. What was amazing was how well his projects turned out with so little preliminary preparation. A sketch, quick measurements, a little math on the materials, and he was ready to go.

"How do you know how to build a whole house?" his young daughter asked.

"I know how to build, so I just sketch out the floorplan and the roof, measure everything, then it's easy to figure out the details as I go," he explained as he worked. She knew better than to ask any more questions.

Always remember that the expression of a trait depends on what other traits a person has, their inner being, and experience. The following is a description of a "pure" expression of this trait without regard for other factors.

Indicates the degree to which a person will process information "on the fly."

The Assumptive person tends to process information very quickly, grasping the gist of what needs to be done, then moving right into action. They believe it's wasted time figuring out every single detail first, because by then, you could have the job done — and they often do. The danger of this trait is they might jump in only half prepared and have to back-track on parts that didn't work.

In conversations they may jump to conclusions about where you are headed and even finish sentences for you if you don't get there soon enough.

Assumptives are built to think on their feet as they are moving toward an objective. They are very future oriented, far more interested in results than in the process, and always prefer facts and figures to theories. Not inclined to sit and ruminate about things, they don't understand or have much patience with people who do. In an emergency that requires thinking on the fly, no one is better at making the seconds count, figuring out solutions as they implement them.

And another hint: don't expect them to read the directions. In fact, don't even give them to an Assumptive, because if you really want those directions read, you'll do well to read them yourself. To an Assumptive, they are simply the object of last resort for when all else fails.

Physical Indicator
- Forehead angles backward from the eyebrows

Behavioral Characteristics
- Mentally quick
- Operate on the fly
- Jump to conclusions
- Prefer summaries, facts and figures to speculation
- Get to the point quickly

Famous People with This Trait
- Liam Neeson
- James Taylor
- Russell Crowe
- John Travolta
- David Letterman
- Jennifer Aniston

Enhanced by
- Low eyebrows
- High ears
- Lots of eyelids
- Coarse skin and hair

Diminished by
- High eyebrows
- Fine skin and hair
- Low ears
- No eyelids
- Down-turned nose

VERTICAL FOREHEAD
"Evaluative"

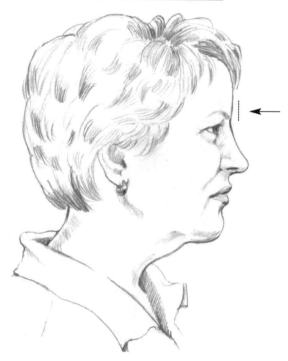

Motto: "I have to think about it."

Margaret had a thing about lists and step-by-step planning. She much preferred to take her time, write it down, plan all the details, and understand thoroughly how it needed to unfold before beginning her work. When her boss pushed her to drop everything and rush into a new project it infuriated her.

"I hate to dash into this without having a plan," she fumed. "It makes me feel like I am flying out of control down a hill and I can't guarantee anything."

"So, what do you need?" he asked.

"Time to understand and plan before I have to start," she said, stating the obvious.

Always remember that the expression of a trait depends on what other traits a person has, their inner being, and experience. The following is a description of a "pure" expression of this trait without regard for other factors.

Indicates the degree to which a person will need time to process information in a linear fashion.

People whose foreheads are straight up in the inch or so above the eyebrows often seem mentally slow. This has nothing to do with intelligence, but rather their style of processing. They are linear thinkers whose mental mode is sequential and evaluative, preferring not to make assumptions but build a complete picture, double check it, then give it time to percolate a bit to be sure it feels right before acting. Some Evaluatives grasp the concept quickly, but aren't comfortable doing anything with it until they have run it through their mental routine to slot all the details and see how it feels.

Respect the fact that while Evaluative thinkers may appear slow, they actually have more brain cells in the prefrontal lobes where advanced mental processes happen. The fact is, they do *more* thinking than the Assumptive person. Their approach is to fully understand a subject before acting rather than assume things that may not be complete or true.

They are often very conscientious as well. What they need is time to think it through, respect for their methods, and an appreciation for the quality and completeness they bring to anything they do.

You sometimes find these people have a great sense of humor that can catch you off guard . . . but more often they get frustrated because they think of the perfect comeback much later.

Physical Indicator
- Forehead is straight up from the eyebrows

Behavioral Characteristics
- Step-by-step thinking
- Process more slowly
- May work from lists
- Pre-plan everything
- Love heroic stories,
- Like to ruminate about things
- Romantic

Famous People with This Trait
- Matt Damon
- Brad Pitt
- Cindy Crawford
- Carolyn Bessette
- Reese Witherspoon

Enhanced by
- No eyelids
- Down-turned nose
- Wide set eyes
- Low ears

Diminished by
- Lots of eyelids
- Upturned nose
- High ears
- Round forehead

SHORT FOREHEAD
"Practical"

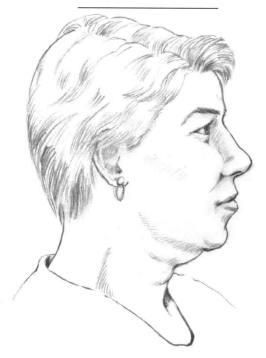

Motto: "To what purpose?"

Ryan and Ellen considered a set of preliminary plans for the kitchen remodel. "We could add a clerestory window in the dining area and vault the ceiling instead of using a skylight. It would look more open," Ryan proposed, "or we could put in two skylights, open up the wall between the kitchen and dining, and add windows over the sink. It would be so much lighter."

"Let's just keep it simple and go with what's here." Ellen interjected.

"But I like to play with the possibilities." Ryan argued.

"To what purpose? This could go on forever."

Always remember that the expression of a trait depends on what other traits a person has, their inner being, and experience. The following is a description of a "pure" expression of this trait without regard for other factors.

Practical

Indicates a need for a practical and utilitarian mental approach.

Practical thinkers are focused on getting the job done in the simplest, most reliable way possible. They are not interested in the theories and concepts unless they are directly tied in to something applicable, and even then, it's usually on a need-to-know basis. The term K.I.S.S. (keep it simple, stupid) was probably coined by a utilitarian thinker who didn't suffer idea junkies gladly.

The good news is, these people accomplish a lot because they are not concerned with figuring out all the possibilities before they proceed. They have a concrete goal in mind and they move toward it in the simplest, most direct route imaginable. Nothing irritates them faster than getting sidetracked into other possibilities when they are trying to just get something done. Also, they prefer the practical to the frou-frou. You'll hear them say things like: "I don't care *how* it works; just work it," or "If you can't *use* it, who needs it?"

These are people who are quite content with what they already know and trust and they dislike being asked to learn new things. They generally detest excess or theoretical information and overly complex ideas, because their mission is to keep things directly applicable and purposeful. You seldom find them in speculative, abstract occupations, preferring a more tangible, "real" line of work.

Physical Indicator
- Forehead is short between eyebrows and hairline

Behavioral Characteristics
- Practical, utilitarian
- Information must be useful and applicable
- Get the job done simply
- Deal in tangibles
- Dislike academics, complex ideas

Famous People with This Trait
- John F. Kennedy
- Madeleine Albright

Enhanced by
- Close-set eyes
- Flat, angled back forehead
- High ears
- Down-turned nose tip

Diminished by
- Roundness to the forehead
- Wide-set eyes

HIGH FOREHEAD
"Abstract"

Motto: "I just like to know."

Brittany started explaining to her dad about "the hundredth monkey" and critical mass in Jung's ideas about the mass subconscious realm we all tap into and are influenced by, when he stopped her.

"What's the purpose of all this stuff?" he wanted to know.

"Purpose?"

"How do you expect to use it?"

"I don't, I just think it's fascinating, don't you?"

Always remember that the expression of a trait depends on what other traits a person has, their inner being, and experience. The following is a description of a "pure" expression of this trait without regard for other factors.

Degree of natural capacity for abstract thinking. They love complex ideas and information.

A really high forehead is a clue that you are looking at an information junkie, a trivia maestro who loves complex ideas and problems. They generally enjoy learning, examining ideas, and may live in a mental realm that is sometimes only marginally connected with physical necessities. So much so that they may have trouble navigating the simpler aspects of practical living, like paying bills on time (or even remembering them), cleaning up a bathroom, or finding their way across town.

Some people push the physical limits, Abstract Thinkers tend to push the limits of the mental. It's as if they have a more complex brain structure and find more complex, even convoluted ways to get from point A to point B. They can make a simple task very difficult, or conversely, they can make the difficult seem simple. Most of the great architectural wonders were designed by Abstract thinkers.

Abstract thinkers can have trouble with practical tasks because it's hard to pull their stratospheric realm down into mundane tangibles. It's also impossibly boring to them. To bring their ideas into fruition usually requires skilled craftsmen and engineers who can manufacture or build what the Abstract thinker can envision, like Frank Lloyd Wright who created soaring, architectural works of art, but some of which didn't function very well.

Physical Indicator

- Forehead is extremely high from eyebrows to hairline (don't confuse it with a receding hairline)

Behavioral Characteristics

- Impractical
- Extremely mental
- Love ideas, theories
- Talk in terms of concepts rather than applications
- Often forgetful in mundane things

Famous People with This Trait:

- Stephen Hawking
- Frank Lloyd Wright
- Beethoven
- Peter Mark Roget

Enhanced by:

- A broad forehead that slopes outward at the top
- A pronounced roundness to the forehead
- No eyelids showing
- Low ears

Diminished by

- Large chin
- Short legs
- Lots of eyelids
- Forehead slopes back
- High ears

CHEEKBONES PROTRUDE
"Risk Taker"

Motto: "Why not!"

Darryn was never one to play it safe and be careful. The thrill of risk filled her with joy and excitement, an adrenalin high. She drove too fast, went places she wasn't supposed to, did things no one else would try and tempted Fate on every turn.

Tom helped her adjust her shoulder harness for her broken arm. "Someday you're going to run out of luck," he cautioned her. "Then what?"

"Then I get to make the ultimate journey and see what's on the other side. We'll all make the journey sooner or later, so why worry?" she said breezily. "Seriously, why live your life afraid to take chances? You miss living!"

Always remember that the expression of a trait depends on what other traits a person has, their inner being, and experience. The following is a description of a "pure" expression of this trait without regard for other factors.

Indicates the willingness to take risks. Needs the stimulation of excitement, adventure, travel.

Often these Risk Takers feel they are "bomb proof" and take chances most of us would rather avoid. And it's not always a physical thrill. It can show itself as a willingness to take a chance on an unlikely love, or a job in a distant city, or becoming an entrepreneur. They have a drive to test themselves through new experiences and generally find routine to be utterly suffocating.

Risk Takers want to get out, see what's happening, what's over the next hill, or around the corner. There is a refusal to be bound by the safe and predictable in life, and sometimes even a need to ride the razor's edge and play with Fate. It's as if the spirit within has to push outward into new and unfamiliar territory. The challenge is to make the exploration meaningful to their lives and to know when and where to set limits.

They crave excitement, travel, variety, and need it to feel alive. Sameness has a quality of the claustrophobic to them and when forced to endure it too long, may take dangerous chances to break free. They have a penchant for breaking rules figuring that "rules were made for people who need them."

Women with these cheeks are seldom content to stay home and tend the hearth. They populate the work world and add to the family income while fulfilling their need for "something happening."

Physical Indicator
- Cheekbones are highly prominent, protruding front and sides

Behavioral Characteristics
- Excitement oriented
- Risk takers
- Need variety
- Love to travel
- Easily bored
- Thrive on change

Famous People with This Trait
- Mariah Carey
- Hillary Clinton
- Cameron Diaz
- Jackie Chan
- Evil Knevil

Enhanced by
- Wide forehead
- Bulging eyes
- Coarse skin and hair
- Meso body type
- Short legs, large chin

Diminished by
- Narrow forehead
- Deep-set eyes
- Fine skin and hair
- Ecto body type

FLAT CHEEKBONES
"Homebody"

Motto: "Why go?"

Jonathan couldn't see any reason to go out. He had been away all day and now he simply wanted to retreat to the seclusion and relaxation of home.

"But Honey, it's Friday night! I want to do something," Joan pleaded.

"To what purpose? I don't want to go somewhere just to go somewhere. I'm where I want to be, home with you. Isn't that enough?"

Always remember that the expression of a trait depends on what other traits a person has, their inner being, and experience. The following is a description of a "pure" expression of this trait without regard for other factors.

Shows the degree of preference for the familiar and routine.

The Homebody is perfectly happy staying put and can see no reason to go somewhere just to go somewhere. An uncle of mine was pushed, shoved, and shamed into driving from the deserts of west Texas to Colorado on vacation. He could hardly wait to get home and when asked how he liked the scenery of Colorado, replied, "What scenery? You can't see anything for those danged trees and mountains."

These people are devoid of the drive for excitement and discovery of new places, and risk taking has no place in their book. They enjoy doing the same things again and again and can see no need for big changes they don't have a compelling reason to make.

A Homebody is like a cat with a territory: they seldom stray beyond their clearly defined boundaries and if pushed past them, will be anxious until they can return to the safety of the known where they feel comfortable and secure with sameness.

Yet, they are willing to stretch when the experience is very important to them, such as a great fan of Simon and Garfunkle who flew to the opposite coast to hear their one reprise concert after twenty years as solo artists. Make a habit of such trips? Never!

Physical Indicator
- Cheekbones appear flat or even sunken

Behavioral Characteristics
- Stay-at-home people
- Enjoy their familiar rut
- Dislike a lot of change and excitement
- "Allergic" to risk taking

Famous People with This Trait:
- Woody Allen
- Prince Charles
- James Stewart

Enhanced by
- Endo and Ecto body types
- Narrow nose
- Small mouth
- Forward set ears

Diminished by
- Coarse skin and hair
- Meso body type
- Wide mouth
- Metal face
- Protruding muzzle and/or eyes

ARCHED NOSE
"Values"

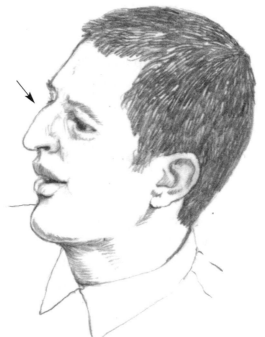

Motto: "Let's negotiate."

Sally came home excited about the promotion she was offered and the salary package. It moved her from the hourly bracket into the salaried but with no overtime pay. Bill turned to his calculator, quickly figured the difference between the hourly and the salary in terms of the number of hours she typically worked.

"They are saving money by promoting you," he said dryly. "Are there any bonuses or other incentives to make it worth it?"

"No, but it is a first step toward management."

"If you want to be a manager, you'd better negotiate a better deal."

Always remember that the expression of a trait depends on what other traits a person has, their inner being, and experience. The following is a description of a "pure" expression of this trait without regard for other factors.

Indicates the degree to which people will push to manifest tangible resources and personal impact in their world.

When people score high in this trait, they are concerned with price and value, enjoy dealing with the financial world, and sometimes treat it like a game they feel compelled to win. Basically, these people are driven by a need to carve a secure place for themselves and their family, and will avidly pursue financial matters to that end. Feeling the weight of responsibility, they often feel unappreciated for how hard they work to provide for others, having taken on all facets of that burden.

Sometimes the drive for financial success is so strong that they can lose sight of human values and needs. It can deteriorate into giving with strings attached, wanting to control all aspects of their loved ones' monetary matters, and failing to really be there in heart and mind. They can appear extremely materialistic, and feel the sting of the accusations, yet fail to understand how their behaviors produce that perception. Some *are* simply materialistic, and tend to grow embittered and cynical with age. Others grow beyond the limitations of a focus on money for its own sake and turn to serving others through their financial expertise.

In the best of worlds, Values people can be incredibly motivated to care for others' needs, and when they are aware of the full spectrum of providing for them, no one does it better.

Physical Indicator
- Nose has a high arch at the bridge

Behavioral Characteristics
- Savvy about money
- Good at bargaining
- Aware of cost and value
- Bargain shoppers
- Adept at arithmetic
- Driven by financial concerns
- Desire for power in the fiscal realm

Famous People with This Trait
- Barbara Streisand
- Aristotle Onassis
- Christina Onassis
- Ross Perot

Enhanced by:
- Thin lips
- Ears that stick out
- Meso body type
- Large nose
- Small irises
- Coarse skin and hair

Diminished by:
- Full bottom lip
- Flat ears
- Large irises
- Small nose
- Endo body type

SCOOP NOSE
"Helper"

Motto: "I like to help."

"I'm exhausted," said Jamie. "I spent the weekend helping Beth with her yard work now that Bob's gone. But I still have to get my own stuff done. "

"Who does your yard since your divorce?" Sue asked.

"I do, silly. You know that."

"I do, and I know your yard is twice as big as Beth's and I haven't seen her over here helping you with yours, ever."

"I know, but it's okay. She doesn't know how and I do."

Always remember that the expression of a trait depends on what other traits a person has, their inner being, and experience. The following is a description of a "pure" expression of this trait without regard for other factors.

94

Degree to which people tend to place human values ahead of financial ones

Helpers are those people who can't seem to say no when others ask for help, or even appear to need help but haven't asked. They volunteer readily and frequently offer open-ended time. When people refuse their help, they may take it as a rejection.

These are tactile people who like to be close to and touch those they like, because touching grounds them emotionally. They may take an attitude of wanting to be close and let happen whatever happens, yet not consider it a romantic commitment, which can lead to misunderstandings.

Helpers tend to automatically take on other people's problems as if they were their own, which side-tracks them from their own concerns. Basically, they may lack a strong instinct for self-preservation, often feeling the pull of another's needs more strongly than their own, doing work without pay, going beyond what is necessary.

Consequently, Helpers often have difficulty on all levels in the realm of receiving because it runs contrary to their internal frame of reference and sense of virtue. To them, virtue is in giving, not in receiving. It can cause them trouble negotiating an equitable compensation for their services. As an adjunct to this, they also may have trouble managing their money since they often lack innate financial savvy and the drive to have wealth.

Physical Indicator
- The nose has an inward curve at the bridge, the so-called "ski nose"

Behavioral Characteristics
- Volunteer readily
- Like to help people
- Upset if people refuse their help
- "Touchy-feely"
- May spend too freely
- Put their own work aside to help others
- Have trouble receiving

Famous People with This Trait
- Bob Hope
- Tom Hanks
- Jennifer Connelly

Enhanced by:
- Large Irises
- Bulging eyes
- Full bottom lip
- Wide set eyes

Diminished by:
- Small irises
- Deep-set eyes
- Wide forehead
- Thin lips
- Close set eyes

DOWN-TURNED NOSE
"Doubting"

Motto: "Show me."

The sales rep made the full presentation, with all the charts, graphs and supporting evidence. Mr. Holden appeared very interested, asked a lot of questions and said it sounded good. So Janet attempted a trial close, asking if he would like to set a date for the delivery.

"Your information was intriguing, but I can't decide on this alone, of course. I'd need to see testimonial letters as well as the scientific data you talked about. Were the tests third party tests and if so, by whom? Also, I'd like to call the labs to verify them. I assume you have phone numbers?"

Always remember that the expression of a trait depends on what other traits a person has, their inner being, and experience. The following is a description of a "pure" expression of this trait without regard for other factors.

Degree to which a person needs full disclosure before trusting or giving acceptance.

When this trait is strong, you can expect a Doubting person to look at new ideas, facts, and people with a healthy dose of skepticism. They consider themselves to be realists, withholding belief and acceptance until they have researched and checked everything thoroughly. They seldom accept anything at face value.

Most have a history of learning through experience that many people can't be trusted. So they have found it is far safer to maintain a personal policy of withholding acceptance and belief until there is proof, using whatever constitutes proof to them. It can take the form of demanding independent studies, third party verification, testimonials, or their own research. Doubting people tend to stay with what they already trust until new information can be confirmed and even certified if necessary.

To other people this attitude may feel stifling, like a wet blanket on the fires of enthusiasm, but to them, it's simply wanting to deal with facts, not claims and quasi facts. Sometimes they may miss out on great possibilities because of their approach.

Doubters like to advise others, feeling that "you should learn from my mistakes." Unfortunately it doesn't work that way. People need to learn from their own mistakes and be allowed to fail and still be supported. After all, we always learn far more from our mistakes than from our triumphs.

Physical Indicator
- The bottom of the nose angles downward

Behavioral Characteristics
- Skeptical
- Mistrusting
- Check facts, references
- Advise people toward caution
- Seldom enthusiastic

Famous People with This Trait
- George W. Bush
- Prince Charles
- Madeleine Albright
- Goran Visnjic (on E.R.)

Enhanced by
- Down-turned eyes
- Close-set eyes
- No eyelids
- Vertical forehead
- Arched or straight nose

Diminished by:
- Large irises
- Scoop nose
- Wide-set eyes

UPTURNED NOSE
"Trusting"

Motto: "I believe."

Sally was beside herself with distress. She had just received an e-mail about the newest pet craze: kitten-in-a-bottle. The missive explained that a breakthrough in science allowed one to take a kitten, put it in a bottle, feed it a liquid diet that softened the bones so the kitten grew into the shape of the bottle. The e-mail said it came with the liquid drops to feed your Kitten-in-a-Bottle.

She called Wenona, who sent her the e-mail, upset almost to tears. "How can people do that? It's horrible! Somebody ought to shoot them!"

"Sally, it's a joke. It's not possible."

"Oh."

Always remember that the expression of a trait depends on what other traits a person has, their inner being, and experience. The following is a description of a "pure" expression of this trait without regard for other factors.

The degree to which a person will accept things at face value and be trusting of others.

An acquaintance of mine loved to make seemingly plausible statements and wait for me to swallow them hook, line and sinker, which I usually did. She would lead me on until it became obvious what she was doing, then give me a hard time about being so gullible. I learned not to believe much of anything she said, regardless of the purpose or intent of the communication. This is typical of the Trusting person: they will trust you too much, but if you burn them, they will never trust you again.

Trusting people prefer to believe that the world is more good than bad and will operate from a space of goodwill and honesty. They are always surprised and hurt when they find it otherwise.

However many times they've been burned, the Trusting person will tend to retain a more open mind and accept things as presented rather than demand proof as a prerequisite to trust or belief. They can get taken in too easily, whether by a lover, a "charitable" scam, or a bad business deal. They have too little "mistrust" filter to draw upon.

Obviously it would be best if they only dealt with honest, trustworthy people, but that's not the way the world is created. So these people need to remind themselves to take full responsibility to check the facts and the people involved before committing to anything major.

Physical Indicator
- The bottom of the nose tilts upward

Behavioral Characteristics
- Overly trusting
- Go by feelings more than facts
- Open minded
- Can be gullible at times

Famous People with This Trait
- Nicole Kidman
- Salma Hayek
- Laura Bush
- Brad Pitt

Enhanced by
- Scoop nose
- Wide-set eyes
- Bulging eyes
- Narrow forehead

Diminished by
- Arched nose
- Close-set eyes
- Wide forehead
- No eyelids
- Deepset eyes

FLARING NOSTRILS
"Independent"

Motto: "My way or the highway."

It took three years and lot of battles before John and Mary hammered out a workable agreement about ownership of jobs around the house. If one claimed the job, the other would step aside and allow them full authority and absolute license to do the job their own way regardless of how hard it was to honor that.

"Actually," John confides, "I have to leave the scene to keep myself from trying to influence or take over the job and that can come to major battles!"

"And the other thing he used to do was sneak in afterwards and redo the job."

"Do you appreciate how badly I still want to?" John asked.

"Yep. As badly as I do." Mary replied.

Always remember that the expression of a trait depends on what other traits a person has, their inner being, and experience. The following is a description of a "pure" expression of this trait without regard for other factors.

Indicates a trust of one's ability to come up with the best solutions and insist on doing it their way.

Independent people hate to be told how to do something. They innately believe their way is the best, or "right" way. In fact, there is such a level of self-trust about it that they have trouble allowing others to do things their own way. They want to take over and be sure it gets done "right," even when it's not their job to do.

Independent people can take the stance of "my way or the highway," which creates problems in relationships of all kinds. They don't usually realize that it shows a lack of respect for the other person. These are not naturally team players and when on a team, they have a tendency to take over the job, go off on their own and do it without allowing input from anyone else, including supervisors. Sometimes they fail to find out all they need to know before proceeding. Typically, their attitude is "I can do it better than anyone else, so why would you want a mediocre job when you could have an excellent one?" This is simply a feeling, not necessarily a fact.

Independent people want the freedom to come up with their own solutions, so as a rule, they are happier working alone. They are seldom satisfied with the way another person does something, which can cause self-esteem problems in others, including their children. To their credit, they are likely to do a good job with little supervision.

Physical Indicator
- The nostrils flare outward from the septum. The greater the flare, the stronger the trait

Behavioral Characteristics
- Won't be told how to do things
- Sure their way is better
- Not a team worker
- Don't delegate well
- Don't accept others' help
- Not open to input
- May try to take over a job and redo it to their own specifications

Famous People with This Trait
- Brad Pitt
- George W. Bush
- Hugh Hefner
- Michael Jordan
- Dame Judith Dench

Enhanced by
- Coarse skin and hair
- Wide forehead
- Large chin

Diminished by
- Narrow forehead
- Fine skin and hair
- Endo body type

SMALL NOSTRILS
"Dependent"

Motto: "I'm not sure I know how."

Elliot studied the dishwasher, read the directions several times as well as the section on installing dishwashers in his how-to book, called his handy-man uncle twice and had at last gotten to the final hookup. But now he was afraid to turn it on without having it checked out thoroughly by someone who knew what he was doing.

"Where are you going?" Marsha asked as Elliot walked out the front door.

"Across the street to see if Scott can come over here and check it out before I turn it on."

Always remember that the expression of a trait depends on what other traits a person has, their inner being, and experience. The following is a description of a "pure" expression of this trait without regard for other factors.

Will mistrust his own solutions and seek input from others.

People with a narrow nose tip don't believe they have the answers. Quite the contrary. They go to great efforts to be sure they are doing something right before they they want to move forward on it. They have even been known to plan a course of action, have all the parts in place and walk away from it when someone tells them it will never work.

I knew a girl in elementary school with this trait who would do the first math problem then sit and wait until the teacher came around and checked it before she would proceed. Mrs. Blythe blew up at her one day and asked, "Why do you always wait for me to check it? Just do them."

"I want to be sure I'm doing it right first," Juanita explained. What she really needed was encouragement to risk making mistakes so she could learn to trust her own abilities. These people have to learn that mistakes are simply part of the path to mastery. Some learn this early, some don't.

When they finally realize that successful people have gotten where they are through daring to try without any guarantees and didn't necessarily know what they were doing either, then they begin to believe in themselves and take more chances with less knowledge.

Physical Indicator
• Nostrils that are narrow

Behavioral Characteristics
• Timid about tackling new jobs without help or direction
• Mistrust their own solutions to problems
• Seek input
• Work well on a team

Famous People with This Trait
• Cher
• Jennifer Love Hewitt
• Christopher Reeve
• Sigourney Weaver
• Gillian Anderson

Enhanced by
• Narrow face
• Ecto body type
• Fine skin and hair
• Low ears

Diminished by
• Wide face
• Coarse skin and hair
• Meso body type
• Metal face type
• High ears
• Prominent cheekbones

FULL UPPER LIP
"Verbal"

Motto: "I love to talk."

Janna was talking when she stepped into the van, talked the entire two-day trip, and continued as they checked into their rooms. Finally Mary's husband had reached his limit.

"Do you always talk this much?" he asked with a slight edge to his voice.

"Yes, and sometimes more. Why?"

"You haven't been silent for more than two minutes in the last two days."

"I must be slipping if I couldn't think of anything to say for two whole minutes. Or maybe that was when I gave you your chance." Janna grinned and kept talking.

Always remember that the expression of a trait depends on what other traits a person has, their inner being, and experience. The following is a description of a "pure" expression of this trait without regard for other factors.

Indicates the degree to which a person will give outward verbal expression to their inner world.

These people have a natural need to give verbal expression to their inner processes. You frequently see a richness to their language, a generosity with words; certainly they are seldom at a loss for them.

There is a strong element of self-discovery in their verbalizing everything. It's almost as if they don't know what they feel until they talk about it. If they are interrupted or asked to be quiet, they may interpret it as a slap in the face, feeling they have been told that they and their feelings don't matter. Or they may laugh it off. They don't realize that often they are not very good listeners but expect others to be.

A gift that this trait sometimes exhibits is the ability to say things in varied ways so they are more clearly understood, which is one of the hallmarks of a good teacher. Also, some writers with this trait have exceptional descriptive abilities.

Generally, Verbal people are unable to think and speak in succinct terms. Their gift is lushness of language and an ability to "fill in the blank spaces" with conversation. When they are anxious or nervous, they have a tendency to chatter.

A famous actress with this upper lip is Julia Roberts and you may remember she didn't want to be limited in her 2001 Oscar acceptance speech. "I'm not through (talking)," she said.

Physical Indicator
- Upper lip is large and very full

Behavioral Characteristics
- Extremely talkative, verbally expressive
- May be repetitious
- Go off on tangents
- Word usage is heavily descriptive, free flowing
- May have a tendency to chatter

Famous People with This Trait
- Julia Roberts
- Maya Angelou
- Muhammad Ali
- Mick Jagger
- Whoopie Goldberg
- Gena Davis

Enhanced by
- Wide mouth
- Protruding eyes
- Wide forehead
- Meso and/or Endo body type

Diminished by
- Small mouth
- Deepset eyes
- Ecto body type
- Narrow forehead

THIN UPPER LIP
"Succinct"

Motto: "Don't waste words."

"How was work today?" Melanie asked her husband.

"Fine."

"And the big presentation to Markson-Bergen?"

"Fine."

"So did you get the contract?"

"Yep."

Always remember that the expression of a trait depends on what other traits a person has, their inner being, and experience. The following is a description of a "pure" expression of this trait without regard for other factors.

Indicates the degree to which a person will naturally limit verbal expression.

Succinct people are masters of the one-word sentence. Dragging a full story out of them is like trying to pull a segmented worm out of its hole — it keeps breaking off into tiny pieces. You would think words cost money and they are on a strict budget. Nothing more than what is needed gets past their lips, and to them, a lavish stream of words is an ostentatious display, an unnecessary waste. They come from the old "speak little and say much" school of communication: that's what they do and appreciate it when others do the same.

The fact is, they mistrust people who are overly talkative and complimentary, suspecting the talkers are trying to con them and would be much more open to them if they would just state the bare facts and dispense with unnecessary chit-chat. If you want to get on their good side, be brief and show them through your actions; then you will be "speaking their language."

Succinct people process their feelings mentally and bottom line it later. Feelings are an uncomfortable subject to them and generally if asked what they feel, they won't know immediately and if pushed to talk about feelings, they can become defensive and cutting. Give them a touch, affection, caring actions, but don't expect verbal expressions of sentiment in return: instead, they'll show you.

Physical Indicator
- Very thin upper lip

Behavioral Characteristics
- Brief to the point of terse
- Dislike small talk
- Detest "chatter"
- Respond to actions more than words
- Mistrust smooth talkers

Famous People with This Trait
- Jay Leno
- Dan Rather
- John Wayne
- Russell Crowe

Enhanced by
- Deepset eyes
- Lots of eyelids showing
- Small mouth, especially strong with both lips thin
- Metal face type
- Ecto body type
- Ears set forward

Diminished by
- Wide mouth
- Endo body type
- Protruding eyes
- No eyelids showing
- Ears set back

FULL MOUTH
"Sensual"

Motto: Sensing is living."

Jane stood in the store skimming a book when her friend Melanie called her over to look at a rack of exotic scarves, wraps, and vests.

"Oh my God! Feel these fabrics," she marvelled. "They make me want to strip down and just roll in them!"

"You wouldn't!" Jane was verging on alarm.

"Only if I thought they wouldn't take me away!"

Always remember that the expression of a trait depends on what other traits a person has, their inner being, and experience. The following is a description of a "pure" expression of this trait without regard for other factors.

Indicates how in-touch the person is with the sensual world.

"That (food) is to die for" is the kind of expression you will often hear from a sensual person. They should know: they live for those exquisite sensory experiences. You find them savoring life — taste, smell, texture — indulging themselves in creature comforts. Sensuals can turn a meal into a religious experience, and they often release the worries of the day with a long soak in a fragrant bath enhanced with soft music, and scented candles. They take time to stop and smell the roses, run their fingers over the smooth glass of a vase, and soak in the full effect of a well designed room.

In relationships, they share feelings constantly, need lots of physical touch, and want to talk about all of it. Like most people, they expect others to have the same approach that they do. Unfortunately, the differences are very real and they may have to learn that a lot of people *don't* relate to the world the same way they do, and they don't want to.

Sensual people are talkative, generous, tactile beings who love to share their feelings, their food, their world. When the mouth is small and the lips very full, they tend to open up with close friends, in one-on-one situations. With a large mouth, they usually thrive in the social scene, enjoy large groups, and like the give and take of group dynamics, and really shine in that environment.

Physical Indicator
- Both lips are very full

Behavioral Characteristics
- Creature comforts are very important
- Love to experience the sensual, from food to fabrics, scents, and sex
- Generous, both tangibly and verbally

Famous People with This Trait
- Mick Jagger
- Angelina Jolie
- Oprah Winfrey
- Sandra Bullock

Enhanced by
- Wide mouth
- Endo body type
- Protruding eyes and muzzle
- Large irises
- Dramatic eyebrows

Diminished by
- Small mouth
- Ecto body type
- Deepset eyes
- Arched nose
- Small irises
- Straight eyebrows

THIN LIPS
"Spartan"

Motto: "Just what's necessary."

Gary and Sue met a new couple at the country club, Marta and Wayland, who belonged to a couples gourmet dinner club. Marta talked about the lavish meals they prepared and invited Gary and Sue to join the new one they were starting the next month.

Sue almost laughed, but merely smiled instead. "Thanks, but I'm not that good a cook," she said by way of declining the invitation.

"Gary, I know you'd love this club. The food is to die for!" Marta insisted.

"No thanks, I can't see going to all that trouble just to cook a meal."

Always remember that the expression of a trait depends on what other traits a person has, their inner being, and experience. The following is a description of a "pure" expression of this trait without regard for other factors.

Degree to which a person will naturally repress verbal expression and sensual indulgence.

The Spartan person doesn't like indulgence in anything and the concept of giving oneself over to sensory experience is generally repugnant to them. They do things because they need to be done, and/or they enjoy it, but they don't do it to indulge the senses. A Spartan takes a short, efficient shower, not a slow, soaky bath. Food is eaten because they're hungry, not to luxuriate in it. They come from a space of self-denial on an emotional level that translates to a real discomfort with any kind of sensual or emotional overindulgence.

If you're married to a Spartan, don't expect a lot of sweet talk. They will show you they care through their actions, not words. In fact, they mistrust flattery and smooth talking, figuring people talk a lot to either cover up something or they're not smart enough to know when to be quiet. They don't suffer chatterers happily. However, if the mouth is wide, they will talk more depending on the circumstances, but it will tend to be about impersonal subjects.

When a Spartan gives a gift, it is for a definite purpose and has been carefully considered. It's a statement of their esteem, not a flamboyant or spontaneous gesture. It might be extravagant in terms of price or quality, but not in the manner of the giving. Their taste generally runs to simplicity, brevity, and understatement.

Physical Indicator
- Mouth is a thin line, no lips showing

Behavioral Characteristics
- Extremely brief
- Not sensual
- Efficiency is important
- Give with much forethought
- Don't like to repeat themselves
- Tend toward self-denial

Famous People with This Trait
- Tom Brokow
- John Wayne
- George W. Bush

Enhanced by
- Deep-set eyes
- Lots of eyelids
- Flat cheekbones
- Meso or Ecto body type
- Forward set ears

Diminished by
- Protruding eyes
- Prominent cheekbones
- Endo body type
- Dramatic eyebrows
- Protruding muzzle
- Set back ears

LOW EARS

"Perfectionism"

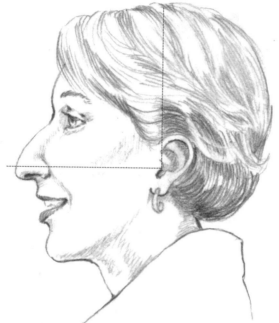

Motto: "It has to be perfect."

Joan planned and coordinated the entire event celebrating her company's twenty-fifth year of operation. Everything fell into place flawlessly except for two glitches: the President's address to the audience ran over by twenty-two minutes, then the Director of Human Resources accidentally picked up two certificates instead of one, and gave both to a recipient. Joan died a thousand deaths when it appeared there was a certificate missing and the Director recognized an honoree with an apology for the "oversight."

"But it wasn't your fault that he picked up two certificates instead of one." her husband tried to console her.

"The whole evening was a disaster. I am so embarrassed."

Always remember that the expression of a trait depends on what other traits a person has, their inner being, and experience. The following is a description of a "pure" expression of this trait without regard for other factors.

Indicates how strongly a person will adhere to his/her own preconceived picture of how things should be.

This trait is a dead giveaway for those people who get on their soapbox about things. They have their standards and don't understand why other people don't live up to them. Even if others don't fulfill their side of a bargain, the Perfectionist will hold his/her own feet to the fire. It's the principle.

This trait can be difficult in relationships, because the Perfectionist frequently dwells on the partner's failings and overlooks the sterling qualities. They get hung up in the "if onlys."

Most Perfectionists can't be satisfied with "good enough:" it sticks in their craw and the flaw is all they can see when they look at it. It may be ninety-eight percent perfect, but that two percent gnaws at them and destroys any joy in a job well-done. This trait can prevent Perfectionists from achieving or performing up to their potential because they tend to pick their work to death or even refuse to put it out there because it doesn't match what they think it "should" be. They set their standards at the highest possible mark and even when they have accomplished something of real value, they downplay the achievement in genuine embarrassment because it falls short of what they envisioned. Often, what they are embarrassed to show, most people would be proud of.

Physical Indicator
- The ears are set very low on the head

Behavioral Characteristics
- Difficulty accepting less than perfect
- Don't feel good about compromising
- Extremely high standards
- Idealists
- Dissatisfied with their own work

Famous People with This Trait
- Alec Baldwin
- Daniel Day-Lewis
- Barbara Streisand
- Meryl Streep

Enhanced by
- Close set eyes
- Down-turned eyes
- High eyebrows
- Fine skin and hair

Diminished by
- Coarse skin and hair
- Wide set eyes
- Upturned eyes
- Low eyebrows

HIGH EARS
"Pragmatism"

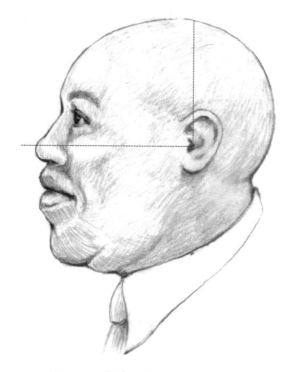

Motto: "That's just the way it is."

"Why can't they make the green level around the cup and center it? This hole has a cockeyed feel to it and it throws my game off every time we play it," Steve complained. "Doesn't it bother you?"

"No sense in getting bothered about it," Michael reasoned. "You can't change it, so you just deal with it and keep moving. Worrying about it is what throws your game off."

Always remember that the expression of a trait depends on what other traits a person has, their inner being, and experience. The following is a description of a "pure" expression of this trait without regard for other factors.

Indicates less concern with perfection and more with progress and getting the job done.

Pragmatic people just want to get the job done and good is good enough; it really doesn't have to be perfect, especially if it's going to slow down the wheels of progress. The act of laboring over every tiny detail, reworking things to the point of utter perfection is like swimming through molasses to them. Just get it *done*.

There is a headlong feel to this trait (especially from a Perfectionist's viewpoint) because Pragmatists want to keep the process moving right along, even if it means compromising on quality and detail. That's more acceptable than the frustration of being stalled or slowed down on a project.

They don't have a preconceived mental picture of how things should be, so they simply deal with what they find and move on. As they see it, investing yourself in an ideal world or an ideal product is a waste of mental and emotional energy. Instead they work to have a good product that will do the job and can be produced in a reasonable time frame. That's all that matters. As far as they are concerned, perfection is a pipe dream and one they are unwilling to spend their time chasing.

In relationships, they are more likely to be appreciative of their partner's good points and not dwell on the minor frustrations.

Physical Indicator
- Ears are set high on the head

Behavioral Characteristics
- Want to keep things moving
- Practical and accepting of what is
- Standards are less important than progress
- Accepting of people the way they are

Famous People with This Trait:
- Minnie Driver
- Angelina Jolie
- Sean Connery

Enhanced by
- Low eyebrows
- Coarse skin and hair
- Wide-set eyes
- Upturned eyes

Diminished by
- High eyebrows
- Fine skin and hair
- Close-set eyes
- Down-turned eyes

ANGLED EARS
"Non-conformist"

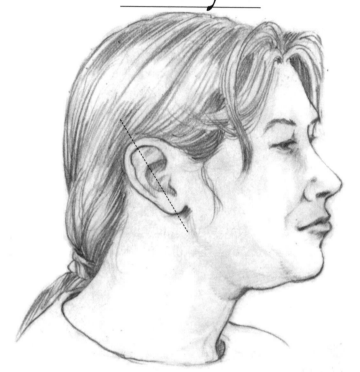

Motto: "I think for myself."

"*The FDA says this is the new food pyramid and these are the kinds of foods you need to be eating,*" *Mary reasoned with her friend, Angela.*

"*Yes, and the FDA said something entirely different up until recently. They will probably change it again in another twenty years. I trust my own research in any area over any bureaucracy any time. Besides, they don't know my body and I do.*"

"*Are you saying they don't do research?*"

"*I have no idea, but whatever research they might be doing doesn't agree with mine.*"

Always remember that the expression of a trait depends on what other traits a person has, their inner being, and experience. The following is a description of a "pure" expression of this trait without regard for other factors.

Shows the degree of independent thinking that may not fit the societal norm.

These people tend to walk to the beat of their own drum and it may not be all that obvious to the casual observer. Yet if you ask them if they like to be different, they will generally toss the question back with, "Doesn't everyone?"

We do all have a need to feel special or unique in some way, but this goes beyond that. It is a need to come to their own conclusions about matters, hold their own ideas regardless of what's acceptable and what's not, and not blindly accept the consensus ideas and attitudes.

Usually it is not blatantly stated, partly because many times it isn't socially acceptable or even safe to hold ideas at variance with the prevailing social attitudes. The other reason is because it's personal and they don't care to discuss it with any but their inside circle; those few like-minded people they have learned to treasure. So while it's not outwardly obvious, nonetheless, it is very important to the Non-conformist to be a "free thinker" and their conclusions will typically diverge from the cultural view in distinctly individualistic and very private ways.

These people often seem to have a subtle difference that may be hard to pin down or define precisely, but they are not your mainstream, socially defined creatures.

Physical Indicator
- Ears slant backward from the vertical. The greater the slant, the stronger the trait.

Behavioral Characteristics
- Think outside the societal norm
- Seem a bit different
- May not discuss their personal views readily

Famous People with This Trait
- Mel Gibson
- Robin Williams
- Ralph Fiennes

Enhanced by
- Rounded forehead
- Eyes set at different levels
- Coarse skin and hair
- Wide face
- Meso/Ecto body types

Diminished by
- Endo body type
- High eyebrows
- Fine skin and hair
- Narrow face

117

VERTICAL EARS
"Traditional"

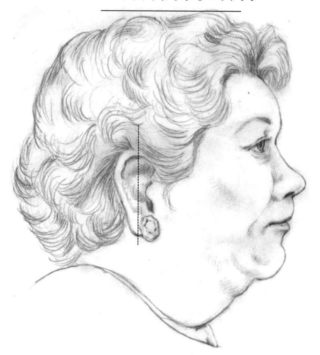

Motto: "I like to fit in."

Ruth simply didn't understand her daughter and her radical ideas. She was actually glad Jennifer lived in another state. It kept her from having to be embarrassed or try to explain her daughter's attitudes and strange eating habits to her friends. When she came to visit, Ruth tried to keep activities within the family and not risk too much exposure. But this time, her best friend had invited all of them over for dinner.

"I appreciate the invitation, Joan, but we're going to Chardonneau's for dinner." Ruth put her off.

"Ruth, are you just hiding her because of her strange ideas?" Joan was always direct.

"Well, yes."

Always remember that the expression of a trait depends on what other traits a person has, their inner being, and experience. The following is a description of a "pure" expression of this trait without regard for other factors.

Indicates a tendency to maintain attitudes and ideas that conform to society's norm.

These people are uncomfortable entertaining ideas and displaying attitudes that are outside the pale. They have a need to live and act within the security and acceptance of a group. To them, it makes sense to go with what has been shown to be correct and proper to the larger society, so they are traditionalists in the strongest sense of the word.

Traditionists don't like to rock the boat or go out on a limb because they basically avoid situations which don't promote group harmony or might isolate them. They prefer to be a functioning part of the whole and sense that you can only do that if you conform to the shape of your place in it. They tend to take the teachings of their culture very much to heart and seldom feel a need to stray beyond it, even mentally.

Radical or new ideas feel threatening to these people and they view them with distaste and distrust. Unlike the non-conformists, these people seldom question the conclusions of whatever authority they give their allegiance to and often consider the tenets of their group to be beyond questioning. Their socially acceptable belief system provides a structure for their lives and they find no reason to go against the flow. As they see it, the questioners are threatening their way of life. They tend to be extremely loyal people.

Physical Indicator
- Ears are vertically positioned, having no slant

Behavioral Characteristics
- Accepting of society's ideas and attitudes
- Dislike radical new ideas
- Support their group
- Stay within traditional boundaries

Famous People with This Trait
- Laura Bush

Enhanced by
- Low-set ears
- Vertical forehead
- Endo body type

Diminished by
- Ecto body type
- High forehead
- Round forehead
- Eyes set at different levels

SET BACK EARS
"Performer"

Motto: "Notice me."

After the first round of drinks was served, the cacophony of voices around the long table and throughout the popular restaurant made it difficult to hear. Gradually, it grew quiet around Don as he continued a hilarious story of his miscommunications with a native Puerto Rican waiter who didn't speak much English and Don spoke even less Spanish.

" 'Uno zapata.' " I yelled at him again and pointed to my empty glass." Don said.

"He was dead drunk" Brett interjected, "and knows less Spanish than a Chinaman."

"That's still more that you know!" Don dismissed him with a look that brought even more laughter. "so anyway the waiter picks up my foot and pulls off my sandal, and bangs it on the table, screaming at me, 'zapata, zapata, zapata!' Then he stuffed it in my mug and stalked out." Don sat with a small grin, nodding. "That's exactly what I thought it meant: shoe." In the roar of laughter, Don was in his glory.

Always remember that the expression of a trait depends on what other traits a person has, their inner being, and experience. The following is a description of a "pure" expression of this trait without regard for other factors.

Indicates a focus on future outcomes and a need for personal acknowledgement.

Like most of the traits, Performer is a mixed blessing. It gives a need to be noticed, and in the extreme, to be the center of attention all the time. It also marks a tendency to seek positions that will put them before an audience and a desire to pursue some kind of public career. Most of the famous people who have sought those positions have these ears. They are usually very good on stage.

Most of their actions are future-oriented and based on what will bring them some manner of recognition. If they are in a group where they can't shine, they soon move on. There's a bone-deep hunger for attention, and when it is denied them, they feel threatened on some level and may react with resentment, jealousy, withdrawal, and/or anger. As children, some may resort to a negative approach if they can't get what they want in a positive way, a behavior they may not outgrow. Some learn positive ways to handle the need, working hard for legitimate accolades and honors.

Many top executives have these ears and it gives them a natural affinity for being center stage, usually developing a finely honed skill at playing to an audience. It is also part of the drive that won them those positions in the first place. When these people learn to hand over the limelight graciously and fully acknowledge others' contributions, they are on their way to mastery of this trait.

Physical Indicator
- Ears are much closer to the back of the head than the front.

Behavioral Characteristics
- Crave attention
- Focus on the future
- Can be adept at handling an audience
- Motivated by recognition
- May lack consideration for others

Famous People with This Trait
- Jim Carrey
- Brittany Spears
- Frank Lloyd Wright
- Frank Sinatra

Enhanced by
- Protruding eyes
- Protruding muzzle
- Upswept eyebrows
- Large irises
- Wide face and jaws
- Meso body type

Diminished by
- Deep-set eyes
- Small irises
- Receding muzzle
- Straight eyebrows
- Narrow face
- Ecto/Endo body types

121

EARS SET FORWARD
"Modest"

Motto: "You are what you do."

There was a job posting on the HR bulletin board that was a perfect match for Angie. She took notes about it, did some research, talked to her friends and husband about the possibility, but didn't turn in her resume until two weeks later. To her dismay, she found that the job had been filled by a coworker who had less experience and training than Angie, but who had jumped on the chance immediately.

"She was in the HR office the day it was posted, and made sure the director of the Traffic department heard about her from three of her friends," Melanie told Angie. "You would have been a better choice. Didn't you apply?"

"I was getting my resume updated and thinking about it."

Always remember that the expression of a trait depends on what other traits a person has, their inner being, and experience. The following is a description of a "pure" expression of this trait without regard for other factors.

Indicates a focus on the past and doing rather than being.

Modest people are generally uncomfortable in the limelight, preferring to quietly sit in the background and observe rather than put themselves forward to be seen. They focus on the past and a job well done, figuring their accomplishments speak for themselves and they need not grandstand. However, if they are passed over, they seldom forget it. That focus on the past can deteriorate into long-standing resentments.

The truth of the matter is, they often fail to speak or act quickly enough to make a difference and are so reluctant to point out their own accomplishments, that they do get passed over. When they learn to speak up quickly and let themselves shine, they are more likely to be seen for what they can do and do well.

Modest people consider everyone in a situation, try to work with others, and seek an equitable solution to disagreements. They make great friends and bad enemies because under the right circumstances, they can hold grudges and may even be vindictive. But if you treat them right, they will reward you with kindness and loyalty.

They have little respect for exhibitionists and Modest people themselves usually aren't exciting, but under pressure they tend to maintain a quiet dignity and give a rock-solid performance.

Physical Indicator
- Ears are positioned in the center of the head

Behavioral Characteristics
- Focus on the past, enjoy history, genealogy
- Seem stodgy, slow
- Hold grudges
- Uncomfortable in the limelight
- Slow to seize opportunities
- Considerate of others

Famous People with This Trait
- Laura Bush

Enhanced by
- Vertical forehead
- Deep-set eyes
- No eyelids showing
- Receding muzzle
- Straight eyebrows

Diminished by
- Angled back forehead
- Protruding eyes
- Protruding muzzle
- Upswept eyebrows
- Heavy eyelids

123

EARS STICK OUT
"Accumulates"

Motto: "What's mine is mine"

Doyle enjoyed every aspect of collecting antique inkwells. He traveled extensively and in his free time, attended every estate sale he could find and hunted through old thrift shops, antique shops, junk shops and even ghost town dumps. He had a special display wall built in his home to house his extensive collection, some quite rare. His fiance, Alice, was showing his collection to her two best friends one day when he walked in. Several were sitting out on the table. Doyle said little, was obviously displeased and didn't leave until every one was back in it's proper place. The next time Alice came over, she found all the doors had newly installed locks.

Always remember that the expression of a trait depends on what other traits a person has, their inner being, and experience. The following is a description of a "pure" expression of this trait without regard for other factors.

Indicates one with a instinctual sense about material values; need for financial security.

People with these ears have a deep appreciation for security and usually put money away. They are seldom big spenders because it is difficult for them to let go of that much money at one time. Usually they are more concerned about making money and hanging onto it, so their major purchases frequently are things that can forward their business or at least, items that will accrue in value. Further aiding this effort is a natural knack for knowing what's likely to help them "turn a buck." Sometimes they are amazingly creative in marketing and business matters.

Accumulative people have a strong attachment to things and an inner connection with their resources, so their challenge is often one of releasing and letting go. Sometimes this may be true for one or two areas, but not hold true elsewhere.

One thing you learn quickly about these people — leave their special stuff alone! It irritates them to have people messing with it and borrowing without asking. And don't ask them to share it.

Frequently people who deal in real estate and tangible goods will have these ears. They are naturally quite savvy about such matters and they often excel in financial fields. The business world is typically easy for them.

Physical Indicator
- Ears stick out noticeably

Behavioral Characteristics
- Like making money
- Need financial security
- Tend to save money rather than spend it
- Dislike people messing with their things
- Can be quite "Scotch"

Famous People with This Trait
- Ross Perot
- Prince Charles
- Madonna

Enhanced by
- Arched nose
- Round forehead
- Close-set eyes
- Wide forehead
- Jutting chin

Diminished by
- Wide-set eyes
- Scoop nose
- Full bottom lip
- Up-turned eyes
- Receding chin

FLAT EARS
"Releases"

Motto: "It's just things."

"I can't believe you aren't upset that Melody lost her wedding band. You must be a saint or something," Judy was amazed at her brother's calm reporting of the facts.

"It's a piece of metal. It can be replaced." Joe shook his head. "I don't understand the hysterics. Is it a woman thing?"

"Not at all," Judy countered. "I misplace my wedding band one time and couldn't find it for three days. Monty was fit to the tied. Doesn't it upset you, even a little?"

"Only if I thought it meant she was trying to lose me, too. Otherwise, no."

Always remember that the expression of a trait depends on what other traits a person has, their inner being, and experience. The following is a description of a "pure" expression of this trait without regard for other factors.

Indicates one who has little instinct for material things and security. May easily overspend.

With these ears, you find people who often don't do the things that will guarantee them financial rewards down the road — it just doesn't occur to them and even if it's pointed out, they don't have the instinct to jump on it. In fact they have to really discipline themselves to do things like save money on a regular basis, and remind themselves not to spend every dollar they have.

Another behavior you'll see is that these people may not go after what is rightfully theirs. I know an artist who did a commission work and after she delivered the painting, found that the man had just filed for bankruptcy. She didn't make any move to regain the painting or pursue getting some payment for the work. She simply let it go.

Unless they have other traits that would counteract it, you will find they might spend their last dime on things they want, need, or on people they love, and worry about it afterwards. They do need and want security as much as the next person, but don't have the built-in instinct for how to do it.

Often they aren't upset if something gets damaged or broken because things are usually not that important to them. They can even lose very important items and not feel emotionally distraught — including a treasured heirloom. They figure most things are replaceable.

Physical Indicator
- Ears are flat against the head, naturally

Behavioral Characteristics
- Not usually shrewd in business
- Spend too freely
- Don't tend to save money
- Seldom go after what is rightfully theirs
- Don't worry about people borrowing their things.
- Not hung up over loss of things

Famous People with This Trait
- Stevie Wonder
- Jay Leno

Enhanced by
- Scoop nose
- Wide -set eyes

Diminished by
- Arched nose
- Close-set eyes
- Rounded forehead

MUZZLE PROTRUDES
"Impulsive"

Motto: "Just do it."

Sallie studied all the TVs on display and asked a few questions, then she bought a twenty-seven inch television set. When she got home and looked at the size of the box in relation to her space, she realized it would be better to return it and promptly did so. As she left the store, she decided she wanted to look at a house that she had driven by the day before, so she called her real estate agent from the freeway to ask if they could meet there.

After seeing the house, she followed the agent to her office and signed a contract.

She likes to tell her friends, "I returned a TV and bought a house on the way home."

Always remember that the expression of a trait depends on what other traits a person has, their inner being, and experience. The following is a description of a "pure" expression of this trait without regard for other factors.

Indicates a natural impulsiveness, a tendency to act before due consideration.

These people will tend to jump in and do things or say things without really thinking them through. Their immediate response is the one they usually go with, sometimes to their regret after all is said and done.

On the other hand, they are great in impromptu situations where they have to ad-lib and think on their feet. Generally, they are going to say just about anything that comes into their heads, which makes them lively and quick-witted companions.

A friend of mine with this trait comes up with great one-liners at the mere hint of an opportunity, like the time the new boss in her office asked her to go get him a cup of coffee. She leveled a look at him and fired back, "What's the matter — those legs painted on?"

The energy is somewhat headlong with this trait and stopping to consider all aspects before acting is more difficult for them. It can feel claustrophobic to have to go through the cumbersome process of looking at everything before proceeding. For them it requires conscious effort to *not* leap first and look later. If you go somewhere with an impulsive person be prepared to switch horses *and* directions in mid-stream several times. Whatever else they may be, they're not boring.

Physical Indicator
- The mouth and chin protrude beyond the forehead

Behavioral Characteristics
- Quick-witted
- Spontaneous
- Impulsive
- Difficulty slowing down to study all aspects before taking action

Famous People with this trait
- Eddie Murphy
- Kristen Johnson
- Jennifer Lopez

Enhanced by
- Angled back forehead or rounded forehead
- Low eyebrows
- High ears
- Protruding eyes
- Short legs
- Large eyelids

Diminished by
- Deep-set eyes
- Low ears
- High eyebrows
- No eyelids

FLAT MUZZLE
"Careful"

Motto: "Think first."

"What do you think of the proposal, Phil? Is it a good business plan?" Randy was excited and it was obvious. This was his first venture as an entrepreneur and he had just unveiled his plans to family and close friends.

Phil sat nodding his head ever so slightly as he mulled over the particulars. "Hmmmph," was all he said.

"You can tell me. I want the feedback." Randy grinned. ""What's my weakest point?"

"Rushing people to give you answers," Phil growled. "I'll let you know when I know."

Always remember that the expression of a trait depends on what other traits a person has, their inner being, and experience. The following is a description of a "pure" expression of this trait without regard for other factors.

Indicates that a person will tend to think before speaking or acting.

People with this trait are naturally a bit cautious and careful about what they do or say. They prefer to consider the consequences before jumping, so you will find them more moderate in their approach. They may not be seen as quick-witted because they will consider the effects first and may decide not to say anything, or to soften the message before speaking.

They are uncomfortable just popping off, and on the rare occasions when they do, it usually feels wrong and forced to them. What you find instead is a more focused, considered comment, which can be devastatingly funny or extremely on-target for the situation.

The Careful person is more cautious overall, but in slowing down to contemplate what they are about to say or do, they are usually more efficient and more considerate of others. There is also a sense of personal boundaries with these people, along with a "don't rush me" air about them.

The beauty of their communication is the judiciousness they bring to it, listening and paying close attention to what's said first, then responding appropriately. You will seldom catch them saying anything they would have cause to regret later.

Physical Indicator
- Mouth and chin are in line with forehead or receding

Behavioral Characteristics
- Deliberate in speech and action
- Think first
- Consider consequences
- Strong boundaries

Famous People with This Trait
- Gweneth Paltrow
- Faye Dunaway
- Tiger Woods
- Alan Greenspan

Enhanced by
- Vertical forehead
- Deep-set eyes
- No eyelids
- Flat cheekbones

Diminished by
- Protruding eyes
- Short legs
- Lots of eyelids
- Angled forehead

JUTTING CHIN
"Determined"

Motto: "Never quit."

Dorothy was often called a bulldog and it fit. When she latched onto some commitment, her jaws locked and she was unshakable.

"They've made it clear you're not wanted on that job. They cut your salary, gave you the worst office. . . why don't you look elsewhere?" Bob asked.

"I have given it my all, I've made a lot of improvements in the system, and I'm not finished. I don't quit." Dorothy said, and that was the end of the conversation.

Always remember that the expression of a trait depends on what other traits a person has, their inner being, and experience. The following is a description of a "pure" expression of this trait without regard for other factors.

degree to which one will hang on to what they consider to be theirs, whether it's a belief, a job, or a relationship.

You can always tell a Determined person: they hang on and hang in there. When they take ownership of a problem, they will stay until they've finished it or the problem is not a problem anymore.

There is a quality of getting the teeth into a commitment and just hanging on, much like a bulldog. To them, it feels like a defeat if they have to let go and walk away. Even more importantly, it is bred in the bone and written on the back of their eyeballs that there is *virtue* in the very act of not giving up, although it may indeed be to their advantage to do so.

The more you try to pull something away from them, the tighter they hold on, and this can include relationships. They really hate to throw in the towel no matter how bad it may be.

People dealing with a Determined person need to understand that this drive to never give up is what motivates them, and you are dealing with a sense of principle and ego investment. It can be difficult to reason with a totally tenacious person who is committed to a course of action. Their whole being can get wrapped up in a small piece of the picture and they take a defeat very much to heart. This can also apply to a verbal battle — they tend to hang in there until they can end it with the last word and feel that they didn't quit first.

Physical Indicator
- Chin bone juts forward

Behavioral Characteristics
- Never quit
- Will hang in there against all odds and reason
- Like to get in the last word

Famous People with This Trait
- Prince Phillip
- Jay Leno
- Kristen Johnson
- Sammie Davis Jr.

Enhanced by
- Wide face
- Meso body type
- Coarse skin and hair
- Flared nostrils
- Pointed or square chin
- Close-set eyes
- Low ears

Diminished by
- Narrow face and nose
- Fine skin and hair
- Ecto/Endo body type
- Wide-set eyes
- High ears

RECEDING CHIN
"Bows Out"

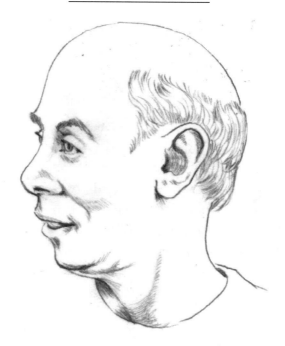

Motto: "Enough is enough."

Barry had been over this territory too many times before. He talked to his manager about the problem, tried to work it out with the other sales rep, but nothing seemed to be getting any better, so he gave his notice.

"I can't believe you just quit your job," said his best friend. "That was good money and a good deal. You could have worked something out."

"Nope. I've been trying to get it worked out for three months. Enough is enough. I'm moving on."

Always remember that the expression of a trait depends on what other traits a person has, their inner being, and experience. The following is a description of a "pure" expression of this trait without regard for other factors.

There is very little ego investment in the principle of never quitting.

The Bows Out person has a built-in tendency to let go of things which makes them easier to deal with than a Determined person. Their biggest challenge is knowing when they really need to hang in there and having the inner fortitude to do it.

This natural penchant for letting things go doesn't mean they can't or don't achieve. It often means they approach things in a less bull-headed way, sometimes taking the maneuver-around-obstacles approach or going-through-another-person method. While the Determined person goes straight after it and defiantly hangs on, the receding-chinned person may try an indirect means if their first few efforts fail, but if that still doesn't work, they will be inclined to let it go and move on.

Often a Bows Out person needs just a little more encouragement in order to keep hanging in there. In a relationship, a partner might have to give more hope of possible solutions, perhaps even help them find solutions, and be sensitive to the inner need to bolt when things don't seem to work.

People with a receding chin really need some light at the end of the tunnel or they may be tempted to walk away. The best part of this trait is the ability to let go and that is a lesson some people never seem to learn.

Physical Indicator
- Chin bone recedes

Behavioral Characteristics
- Not a lot of staying power
- Easy to deal with
- Not invested in "never quit"
- Ability to let go

Famous People with This Trait
- Don Knotts
- Steven Van Zandt
- Prince Edward

Enhanced by
- Narrow face and nose
- Protruding eyes
- Lots of eyelids
- Angled-back forehead
- Close-set eyes

Diminished by
- Wide face
- Coarse skin and hair
- Flared nostrils
- Wide-set eyes
- Vertical forehead
- Low set ears

WIDE JAWS
"Dominant"

Motto: "I make things happen."

"You seem to like to be in control of a situation," I mentioned to Bart.

"No, that's not strong enough." he grinned. *"It's like this: if I walk into a room and see that there's no way I can control the situation, I leave."*

"On really! And in your adult life, how many times have you left?"

"Twice. One was dealing with the Undersecretary of War."

Always remember that the expression of a trait depends on what other traits a person has, their inner being, and experience. The following is a description of a "pure" expression of this trait without regard for other factors.

Indicates one who automatically takes charge in any given situation.

Dominant people tend to assume control of a situation whether they actually have the authority or not. They can't seem to sit back and let things happen without attempting to exert power and influence over the proceedings, whether it's the local meeting of the Spoof Club or a Senate investigation. They naturally assume command and are especially prone to do so when the person in charge fails to use a firm hand.

They seldom back down when challenged, and may make a show of rage, raising the volume of the voice to intimidate. It's all a matter of not losing face. They tend to rise to positions of power by virtue of assuming it. When Dominant is combined with other strong traits, these people are natural leaders. If it isn't supported, they may simply try to control matters without real leadership, and have inborn "push back" when challenged or pushed.

These wide-jawed people usually hate to admit they are wrong or don't know something. They may try to face people down or bluff it. There is a natural drive to claim authority and dominion in their world, yet Dominant people can often be more effective when they learn that by being more vulnerable and low key, they will attract people to support them instead of moving in with their take-charge approach. And when all is said and done, they *do* make things happen.

Physical Indicator
- Jaws are as wide as or wider than the forehead

Behavioral Characteristics
- Take control
- Naturally try to lead
- Take the offensive when challenged
- Seldom admit they are wrong or don't know

Famous people with This Trait:
- Julia Louis-Dreyfuss
- Dick Cheney
- John Travolta
- Donald Rumsfeld
- Sean Connery
- Salman Rushdie

Enhanced by
- Wide forehead
- Coarse skin and hair
- Flared nostrils
- Meso body type
- Metal or earth face
- Close-set eyes

Diminished by
- Fine skin and hair
- Narrow forehead
- Ecto body type
- Wide set eyes
- Upturned eyes

137

POINTED CHIN
"Opposition"

Motto: "Don't tell me what to do."

Emma ran upstairs to her room with the new comforter. On the way, she pulled matching lavendar sheets out of the linen closet, laid them on the chair and began stripping her bed.

"Honey, I think those lavendar sheets would be perfect," Her mother called from downstairs. "Why don't you put them on your bed?"

Emma closed her eyes and heaved a silent, angry sigh. "No, Mom," she called back, "I'm gonna use the green ones." She picked up the lavendar sheets and exchanged them.

Always remember that the expression of a trait depends on what other traits a person has, their inner being, and experience. The following is a description of a "pure" expression of this trait without regard for other factors.

Indicates an instinctual opposition to directions from other people.

People with this trait have a built-in, knee-jerk reaction against being told what to do, pushed, or manipulated, however benign the intentions. Their resistance is an unconscious emotional reaction to anyone trying to direct their efforts or any aspect of their life. Often you will see a passive resistance, such as doing something else instead or simply not do it at all.

This trait has a quality of defending boundaries rather than an aggressiveness. People with wide jaws feel their power and try to take over. People with these narrow jaws feel somewhat powerless and fight being taken over. Pressure and stress builds up pressure in the body, and Oppositional people tend to either get sick or explode. What they need is respect, first and foremost. When forced, a person with this trait may knuckle under, but they will do it with extreme resentment and they won't forget or readily forgive. If they don't understand this trait, they can be manipulated in reverse, and lose energy fighting petty battles.

Probably half of all children have this trait. It seems to be a part of the essential process of individuation and becoming their own person. For some people it is a never-ending struggle, and yet when people become more sure of who they are, realize their own strength and individuality, they often outgrow the need to oppose and it softens.

Physical Indicator
- Chin or jawline is pointed

Behavioral Characteristics
- Stubborn when pushed
- Resist suggestions
- Can be passive-aggressive
- Don't like to confront directly
- Build resentment under pressure, then explode or get sick

Famous People with This Trait
- Julia Louis-Dreyfus
- Jennifer Love Hewitt
- Kifer Sutherland
- Russell Crowe
- Liza Minneli
- Prince William

Enhanced by
- Narrow forehead
- Close-set eyes
- Ecto body type
- Deep-set eyes

Diminished by
- Wide-set eyes
- Large irises
- Protruding eyes
- Wide mouth
- Endo body type

Tim

Part IV
USING THE INFORMATION

One of the things you learn rather quickly when reading faces is the importance of assessing how the traits interact. We touched on this on pages 14 and 15, and now let's look at ways to work with it.

When you first start learning to read faces, it's easy to get lost in all the details. So it's a good idea to work with a system for reading a face. What I like to do it look at it in terms of how they are likely to respond on an overall basis.

To do this, I look at four things. First, establish how adequate they feel (the width of the forehead) in a new situation. Second, assess the skin and hair texture for how adaptable they are to their physical environment. Third, check the width between the eyes for how quickly they respond to stimulation, and fourth, assess the height of the ears for how emotionally invested they are in their beliefs.

With these four factors, and using high, low, and medium, you have a good basic starting point. Choose half a dozen people and try this. You only need to work with a few to begin to get a feel for it.

Note these four traits, write down the keywords about each trait, then you can mix and match to make sentences about the different combinations. This gives you a strong sense of basic approaches. When you have a real feel about the basic drives, then you can begin adding other traits to the mix, seeing what makes these stronger and what would soften the effects. On some people, you will see conflicts in the personality; or conversely, with everything pointing the same way, you begin to understand why he or she comes across as such a strong personality.

When there are a lot of strong traits, this contributes to a strong personality (and easy to read). They tend to be more polarized in their responses to life and therefore are more predictable.

When a lot of the traits are in the middle, the person will be more balanced and have broader responses to life, so it's harder to peg them. What you have to do is find those few traits that are very strong, and know that these will tend to define the personality. The other thing to be aware of is that they can adapt to a situation better than a lot of people.

On the following pages are two examples of this method to get you started.

Example A:
- ❑ Wide forehead
  - feels adequate, not afraid of the new
  - learns hands-on, is thorough
  - thinks big, needs a challenge
  - needs to feel needed
  - respects strength
- ❑ Coarse hair/skin
  - runs over obstacles
  - more is better: quantity over quality
  - lets it all hang out
  - takes a lot to get under the skin
- ❑ Close-set eyes
  - reacts immediately,
  - can't relax till finished
  - wants everything done now
  - keeps everyone in line, conscientious
  - hard to please, intense
  - focus on specifics, one thing at a time
- ❑ Low ears
  - passionate about beliefs
  - won't compromise ideals
  - high standards, perfectionistic

As an immediate assessment, you notice two traits that are oriented to thinking and acting on a grand scale and two traits indicative of very high standards and perfectionism. You quickly realize this is a person who is likely to be self-motivated, not a slouch and not deterred by other people's opinions. Probably some good leadership potential.

Then if you take keywords and play with them, you flesh out that immediate assessment with such statements as:

142

— "Learns hands-on, feels equal to almost anything, is hard to please and perfectionistic."

—"Likes to live bigger-than-life and does it with passion."

—"Holds everyone to high standards in his drive through obstacles.

—"Impatient, intense, focused on specifics, uncompromising."

—"Needs to feel needed and so tends to keep everyone in line with a focus on specifics."

Do you notice how you begin to get a picture of this person's method of operation? You soon find yourself reading between the lines and connecting dots with things that add up. For example, the need to feel needed and wanting to keep everyone in line could mean tending to closely monitor anyone working with or under him to ensure that his high standards are met. He probably won't accept excuses.

Another direction you can take this is to understand that the innate self-confidence factor (wide forehead) with its approach of hands-on learning without fear, means he is likely to have little patience with or respect for more timid people; those who hesitate in the face of big challenges, are afraid to tackle new things, and react in fearful, sensitive ways. He might tend to dismiss them, try to push them beyond their limits, or run over them. All of these are possible. When you understand these tendencies, you look for other traits that corroborate these or mitigate against them.

For example, flared nostrils, a big, square chin, wide jaws, small irises, and an aim-focused forehead would all add to the intensity of the drive. On the other hand, a more narrow nose tip; a smaller chin with roundness, larger irises; more narrow, rounded jaws; a gently rounded forehead will all soften the driven quality.

Now let's look at another basic mix.

Example B:

❑ Narrow forehead
- feels inadequate, must prepare
- afraid things won't work
- more sensitive to others' feelings
- may not be thorough
- uses knowledge to gain confidence

❑ Coarse hair/skin
- likes to live big, think big
- more is better: quantity over quality
- lets it all hang out
- takes a lot to get under the skin

❑ Close-set eyes
- reacts immediately
- can't relax until finished
- do it now, do it right
- keeps everyone in line, conscientious
- hard to please, intense
- focus on specifics, one thing at a time

❑ High ears
- will compromise to make progress
- pragmatic
- accepting of reduced standards
- focuses on immediate goals

An immediate assessment gives you the pragmatic approach of reduced standards with the coarse skin and hair which concerns itself with quantity over quality. Then add the feeling inadequate, fearful part (narrow forehead) to the close-set eyes (can't relax, intense, reacts immediately) and you have a more defensive person who may think bigger than he acts.

Taking the keywords and building with descriptors give you:

— "Uses knowledge to gain confidence, wants immediate action and progress, so may compromise thoroughness, standards. "

— "Worries about what could go wrong, prepares to avoid failure, reacts immediately, is intense and critical.

—"Thinks and dreams big but fears tackling too much at once, so may move forward one thing at a time, focusing on the immediate steps and short-term goals."

— "Won't tackle big challenges without knowledge, can't relax until it's all finished."

As you can see, there's a number of qualities that can have the effect of cancelling each other out, or setting up conflicts, such as "may not be thorough" and "willing to make compromises; accepts reduced standards" as opposed to "conscientious" plus "do it now, do it right." Two traits, the coarse skin and hair plus the high ears reduce the perfectionism of the close-set eyes. On the other side of the coin, the narrow forehead, (fearful and needing approval) coupled with conscientiousness and the need to do it right brings out some drive for perfection. What often happens is they wind up functioning more like in the middle, exhibiting behaviors from both sides at different times. In these cases, you will find *other* strong traits have a much greater effect on outward personality and the behaviors they exhibit.

Considering that, now you want to assess other traits to see what effect they will have. For example, let's say he also has wide nostrils (independent), a big, square chin (physical stamina), low eyebrows (informal, "good enough"), a deeply angled-back forehead (goes straight for the objective), and small irises (dispassionate). All of these will enhance the coarse hair/skin approach. It makes him less sensitive to others, less concerned with perfection and other's feelings, do it my way, and even quicker on the uptake. What you'll have is someone who feels he has to get things done immediately, so is likely to be more easily satisfied with "good enough," and may be defensive to boot.

Now let's take the opposite additional traits and apply them to the same basic four. Suppose this person has narrow nostrils (seeks input, doesn't trust own abilities), a small chin (not physical, little stamina), high eyebrows (discriminating, quality-oriented), a vertical forehead (sequential thinking, needs time to evaluate things), and large irises (emotionally responsive and expressive).

The narrow nostrils, small chin, large irises, and straight-up forehead will enhance the effect of a narrow face and make the person very conscientious, prone to feeling guilty, and doubles the need for approval. Combine that uptightness with the high eyebrows of pickiness and its quality-oriented nature and you have the "do it right" expression of those close-set eyes strongly enhanced.

You can see how each trait has an effect on the over all expression and nothing stands alone. You have to take all the elements into account when reading a face and learn to assess how the traits will express together. All that said, you will find that most of the time, strong traits tend to dominate the personality and reading just those will give you a high degree of accuracy in a limited arena ninety-five percent of the time.

What about surgery?

I read one woman at a party who had the cutest little upturned, scoop nose you ever saw, and I said that she was a natural helper who might not be too aware of cost and value, but focused more on the people values.

She frowned. "No, I'm not like that at all. What part of my face are you reading?"

"Your nose."

"Oh," she leaned forward and confided, "I had a nose job a few years ago. I hated my big hook nose."

"Well, that changes the picture," I smiled. "In that case, I venture to say you are extremely aware of cost and value and are good at the administrative side of things. Personally, you're probably a bargain shopper, like to negotiate a deal and when you do, it makes your day."

She started laughing. "Now, that's me!"

After several of these encounters, I have concluded that the inner self is subject to change only from within. If you alter the face through surgery, you simply alter the face, not the inner self. Life experiences and choices can change us enough that it manifests outwardly, but it generally doesn't work the other way around. There are exceptions of course. A friend of mine told me that she had her deeply receding chin enhanced and she found she had changed in the the years since, becoming more determined and self-confident. Any factor that affects our sense of self has the capacity to change us; from our self-perceptions to parenting, to peer pressures, to choosing how we see things. And whatever changes us has the possibility of changing our faces.

Then you might consider that: a) people are complex, b) the only constant is change, and c) there are over six billion of us around. So as a face reader, you need never be bored!

What about genetics?

To the degree that you look like your parents, you will have traits in common with them. If you have the eyes like your mother's, you will have the same approaches they indicate. If you have your father's forehead, you

147

will have the same kind of thinking process. That doesn't mean you will reach the same conclusions, only that you will process information in the same basic style, whether it's linear, intuitive, or assumptive.

Sometimes this sameness is a wonderful thing; sometimes it causes people to come to loggerheads because both might be equally stubborn or equally determined to do it their own way, and so on. But we can understand the other person more easily when we have the same trait.

Knowing this can help you find new ways to deal with situations as they arise. Ideally, this would require compromises and mutual respect. When using face reading to its maximum benefit, you get to work on yourself and understand your other family members.

In Conclusion

Face Reading is a wonderful tool with many applications, but most of all it is a gift to enrich your life. Even if you never use it beyond an attempt to see what's on your own face, it can give you validation about your inborn tendencies and perchance a greater self acceptance.

If you choose to pursue the art and use it in your daily interactions, it will at the very least give you insights into natural behaviors and broaden your approach. At best, you will be able to interact and communicate more effectively, deepen your acceptance and tolerance of others, and have much joy and satisfaction in perceiving people more realistically and appreciatively. And somehow there's a measure of redemption in seeing the humor of people being themselves so we can detach from the need to take it personally and simply enjoy the ongoing drama that surrounds us.

Part V
SAMPLE
READINGS

O on the next few pages, there are two sample readings. Study the pictures, first see what traits you find and what that means about the person, then read the information and see how close you came. These readings are valuable in that they show you how you can combine traits to get a deeper, clearer understanding.

You will notice that I don't start at the same point on a face. You want to look for dominant traits to begin the reading, then add nuances based on what else is present. Remember, traits that are in the middle won't tell you definitive things about the person, but rather show areas where they will tend to have a more moderate approach.

I've used two famous people so you can read up on them to check on at least some of the validity of the information.

Mohandas K. Gandhi, Age 27

Mohandas Gandhi is a fascinating study in light of his life story, knowing what he accomplished and the odds against him. The picture above is drawn from one taken of the young Gandhi in South Africa. The second drawing is of Gandhi as most of us remember him; as a wise elder.

There is an incredible combination of traits shown on his face and head that indicate a fighting spirit with the will to back it up and the uncompromising devotion to his ideals. The shape of his head indicates the capacity to maintain consistent action toward long-range goals, with the drive to push through obstacles in the moment and the capacity to rise to the occasion and find within himself the wherewithal to face life's challenges head-on. The other traits in this power combination include a square fighter's chin, take-charge jaws, flared nostrils of an independent problem solver, low ears for a depth of passion about his beliefs, the wide face of inner fearlessness and risk-taking cheekbones. Then he has other gifts that gave him the charisma and timing to turn mobs into the mass movements of political power.

Now let's look more in-depth at the traits and how they interact to give us a glimpse of a man who changed history.

In the width of his face, we see an innate feeling of adequacy which allowed him to face his world undaunted by the unknown and untried. This trait means he would need challenges, would learn quickly if he set his mind to it, and in all matters he committed to, he would be thorough. Notice the prominent cheekbones (risk taking). In his own writings, we know he was driven to experiment with many approaches to life in his youth, stepping outside the bounds of his society, suffering great guilt because of it, yet needing to risk it anyway. Although he had great fears (including a terror of public speaking) he never let them stop him, such as deciding at age nineteen to study law in

England and proceeding to do so over the protest of his entire family, none of whom had ever been to England. He faced down his own shyness and feelings of strangeness in the milieu of English society to stay and successfully complete school and the bar exam. (And while he was at it, he also made powerful connections to the avant garde thinkers in England, occasionally writing for their publications, connections that would serve his causes well in future years.)

His coarse hair and skin show he was ruggedly built with the capacity to think and act in bold and daring ways, could readily withstand extremes in the environment, not be bound by others' approval, and had a high pain threshold. You could see this trait at work (thinking and acting in bold ways) with his decisions to take on entire governments and his ability to withstand the rigors of being held in jails, fasting, and working long and hard as we know he drove himself to do.

The wide, square chin indicates a fighter who could be contentious (even while holding a gentle demeanor), questioning status quo attitudes, and taking the battles to court and to the streets. While it's not the long chin of great physical stamina, he had physical drive through other traits. The smallness of the chin gave him a more mental approach, rather than a physical one — the iron-fist-in-a-velvet-glove syndrome.

Another power trait is his strong jaws, giving a "take charge" tendency which means he would step up to the plate and go to bat for his causes. The flared nostrils show him to be independent, trusting his own instincts in problem solving. He preferred to do things his way and generally did. The low-set ears show his devotion to his ideals and the passion he brought to them. He could not be bought, nor could he be bullied into capitulation. Consider all of the above in conjunction with those prominent cheekbones and you have great personal strength, ideals, and drive coupled with a willingness to take personal risks.

Gandhi was also blessed with other gifts that added grace and finesse to his powerhouse combinations. His rounded, sloped-back forehead shows a quick mind that tends to move immediately toward his mental objective, along with some degree of practicality. The curve of his forehead shows originality and conceptual, intuitive thinking in his mental approach, while the flatness in the center shows an information gatherer. He read widely in matters he needed to understand and sought information and ideas that would further his purposes and feed his own ideas.

If you examine his eyes closely, you will see some strong variations. One is wide set with a lot of eyelid showing, and the other is more close-set, with very little eyelid showing. These gives him two modes and some unpredictability: one (wide-set, lots of eyelids) a more accepting person with a broad view, a dislike of pettiness, and a willingness to tolerate people and situations for some time before reacting, plus an ability to cut to the heart of a matter and act immediately. The other mode (close-set eye, almost no eyelid) is a drive to handle matters immediately and correctly, and to probe deeply into detail so he could speak with full knowledge on matters. His history shows several combinations of these in his methods of operation.

His eyebrows arch upward from the bridge of the nose, so he had an innate capacity to dramatize a situation and create a desired effect whether with his words, his delivery, his actions, or his timing and often with all of them. Think of his walk to the sea with all the masses watching, and his stooping to pick up that handful of salt with which he declared war on the British Empire. He had a natural affinity for maximizing the drama inherent in a situation.

The prominent, out-turned ears show an awareness of what would be to his financial advantage (he was a highly successful lawyer in his thirties and forties) and they also gave him an acute sense of hearing. His ears further indicate he was not a man seeking the limelight, nor did he fear it.

One of Gandhi's most amazing personal feats was the subjugation of his enormous sensual appetites. The very full lips give natural generosity, an innate ability with words, and a strong appetite for the sensual world — taste, touch, texture, and the sexual. Yet as he matured, he fasted frequently, both for personal, spiritual purposes, and for political leverage, and he took a personal vow of celibacy. In the volumes written about him and by him, there are three things he claimed he was obsessive about: truth, diet, and sex. He also had a rather wide mouth, the mark of an extrovert who flourished with human interaction. Take these facets and realize this man chose asceticism, celibacy and fasting as cornerstones to his lifestyle. With the all the powerful traits he could bring to bear on matters of will, we can certainly understand how he could maintain such a drastic path.

Gandhi is a lesson in working with one's traits, choosing what to use, how to use it and what to overcome. He was a man who used his gifts in powerful ways, and chose how he would engage his natural abilities and to what purposes and still be as imperfect as any of us.

Carl Jung noted that a person's life is reflective of the person.

Whether we look at Gandhi's life as a natural reflection of his traits in action or consider that the traits were the tools he could bring to bear on his choices and direction, we must acknowledge that he was uniquely endowed for the extraordinary life he composed out of his quite common circumstances.

Oprah Winfrey

Oprah Winfrey is in the unique position of breaking down barriers, wielding a lot of power, making more money than most white men, and doing it as a black woman both contributing to and riding a cresting wave of change. That's not to say she has done it alone. That's part of the genius of agents of social change: they know how to read their social milieu, how to harness the power of many, and they have the vision to carry it forward. She has been at the right place at the right time with the right stuff and the right people to make it happen. So what makes Oprah who she is?

Many things, some of which are the natural traits she was born with and of course, she too, has had to learn to make choices in how she uses her natural abilities. but all in all, she is marvelously endowed for the lines of work she pursues as talk show host, actress, and producer. Let's look to her traits for an explanation of how she does it so naturally.

Most people lack the confidence or ability to ever step in front of a camera and host a show, let alone produce their own. It takes an unusual combination of traits to do it successfully. Some of these include a wide face (feeling adequate), Endo/Meso body build (dynamo energy plus natural empathy), relatively coarse skin and hair (thinks big, goes for the gold), wide jaws (takes charge), large head (relentless drive toward goals), set-back ears (showmanship, at home in front of an audience), full upper lip (gift of gab), and a protruding muzzle (spontaneous).

Let's look at these "CEO traits" more closely, then we'll look at her other gifts and finally traits that are challenges and how she has worked with and through them to get where she is today.

Indicative of an innate trust of her own abilities and a need for something to challenge her is the wide forehead, the sense of Adequacy. It also shows a tendency to focus on why something can succeed rather than dwell on why it might not. This helps spur her dreams with a positive attitude about her chances of accomplishing them, and we know that beliefs and expectations are powerful. Oprah's body build shows a combination of Endo and Meso body types, giving her great drive, energy, and stamina to back up her acceptance of challenges. Her somewhat coarse skin and hair shows Toughness, a tremendous enjoyment of the physical world, and adds even more stamina plus a certain invulnerability to the environment. Tough people have the capacity to drive straight through obstacles and not get hung up in the minutiae or in what other people think.

The large size of her head is legendary and points to a lot of mental energy backed by a relentless drive, what I call "do something" energy;

always furthering her ideas rather than just thinking about them, fueling her ambitions with concrete steps toward achievement. Helping her get a handle on her projects is a set of wide jaws which means that Oprah doesn't wait for someone else to make things happen: she takes charge and sees that they get done. Another nice little plus this trait offers is the chutzpa to bluff her way through difficult situations, even when she is shaking in her boots. You could call it having guts. And she's got another variety: a natural gut-trust intuition that helps guide her actions, thanks also to her Endo/Meso body type.

All of that is what combines for the incredible drive and energy that underpins Oprah. Some of the more subtle gifts show in her nostrils and the placement of her eyes. Oprah is open to input in her approach indicated by the smallness of her nostrils. This means she will seek input from those she trusts and is willing to hear suggestions and other people's ideas rather than always assume her own solutions are the best. Also broadening her scope of responses is the fact that she has one eye almost close-set and one eye wide-set. The close-set eye is on the right side, her professional, take-myself-out-into-the-world side. So in her professional life, she is more intense, demanding, perfectionistic, notices details, and does not procrastinate. On her left side, the personal self, she is more laid back, big-picture, and easy going, except when she's under stress, then she moves into the other mode of "do it now, do it right." And of course, as an undercurrent to all of this is her demanding physical drive that seldom allows her to simply sit still. She has an insatiable need to be doing and because of her eyes and nose, she is more inclusive in getting it done.

The next set of traits have to do with her ease on stage. Some people take to working in front of the cameras like a duck to water and Oprah fits in this category. The combination of traits that give her this legitimate desire includes first of all, Performer, indicated by her ears set toward the back of her head. This trait affords her an inbred showmanship capacity, a sure instinct for playing to an audience and taking them where she wants to go. When you add a natural ability as a storyteller (full upper lip), spontaneity (muzzle protrudes) with quick, intuitive mental processing (round forehead), you get someone who is exceptional at ad-libbing, a natural talk show host. She is also rather discriminating (fairly high eyebrows) and has dispassionate eyes (irises are relatively small), which give her the capacity to keep strong personal boundaries, maintain good taste, and delve into highly emotional topics without totally losing her composure. Add still another piece to that mix with her healthy dose of the Endo body type, and you see her natural rapport with people, an empathetic host who is very relationship-oriented. Fortunately, the dispassionate eyes temper the empathy that prevents her from going off the deep end into mawkish sentimentality and also contributes to her business savvy.

Among her challenging traits are Sensuality (full lips) and the high degree of Endo body type. Both of these incline her toward a natural enjoyment and desire for food — luxuriating in taste, touch, texture, with an affinity for the creature comforts. Her battle with her weight is a battle with her authentic self. It is far more difficult for an Endo body type to refrain from eating and harder for them to not gain weight than any of the other body types. Endos have a natural, intense enjoyment of food, deeply enhanced by an appreciation for the ceremony, and social rituals around eating. (Endos also are built to assimilate — in other words, gain weight.) Her full lips practically double this inclination. When you then consider the effect of her relatively coarse skin and hair, you realize she thinks and likes to live in larger-than-life terms, and when she likes something, more is better. The fact that she has managed to curb her natural tendencies as well as she has is much to her credit. She should never compare herself in her efforts to take off the weight to people who don't face the same challenges she does. They can lose more with less effort.

Among her other challenges are those relatively straight eyebrows which show an appreciation for the world of the arts, a need to be surrounded by beauty, and a craving for harmony and balance in her environment. There is a tendency to do nice things for others, wanting to bring beauty and peace to her world, and a strong desire for acceptance. It would be easy for her to get lost in a world of pleasure, and not want to deal with the ugly, inharmonious side of life. It indicates a tendency to try to escape a world that isn't pleasant plus a difficulty in dealing with too many changes too fast. It tends to throws her off balance. Combined with the natural Endo need for acceptance and love, it can be difficult to handle, especially when one is young and untried. (The Toughness and physical drive helps here.)

Certainly Oprah's childhood was rife with these kinds of conditions and it could have easily destroyed any chance for success in life. Fortunately, at a crucial point, she was sent to live with her father and stepmother who were very firm and helped her get her feet back under her. A number of her power traits also helped counterbalance this tendency, not the least of which is an intuitive, rather practical mind which is poised between extremes. She is intelligent and ambitious without getting muddled in sterile intellectualism and she is grounded by the practical without being harnessed to it. The rounded shape shows intuitive thinking that grasps whole concepts quickly and easily and can be quite creative and original. She's not at a loss for ideas.

All in all, Oprah is a testament to the power of choice we all have, and a great role model for using what one is naturally endowed with to explore this gift of being human.

Appendix A

Face Reading Time Line
in Western History

The following table of the history of face reading in the Western tradition only is designed to easily place the major contributors in a time frame and in relation to each other. It is also conceived as a visual aid in tracing the development of face reading and other closely related theories through the centuries.

700 BC	**Homer** (circa 700 BC), Greek poet includes very direct descriptions conjoining physical structure to behaviors in his narrative poems, _ILLIAD_ and the _ODYSSEY_.
500 BC	**Pythagoras** (581—497 BC), wrote about face reading, used it as part of his interview process for acceptance into his school.
400 BC	**Hippocrates**, (460—377 BC), Greek physician acknowledged physiognomy in his practice, developed his own four temperament types.
300 BC	**Plato** (circa 427—347 BC). The most famous Greek philosopher whose ideas have affected all of Western thought, wrote specific descriptions of physical features that would qualify their owners for various occupation and even discussed psychological principles long before psychology was a separate study.
	Aristotle (384—322 BC), advanced his theory of physiognomy in both his _History of Animals_ and the treatise, _de Animalibus_
100 BC	**Roman Empire** Face reading was an honorable profession during Roman times, with a sophisticated system of delineating character.
100 AD	**Galen** (c.150) Like many educated and curious men after him, Galen performed autopsies, dissecting the human anatomy and postulated that

160

the brain controlled man's innate character and that the skull shape and size was a reasonably accurate indication of brain proportions.

Rhazis (c.860— c.925), innovative Persian physician, wrote about character judgement, refining Aristotle's ideas.

Avicenna (980—1037), **Averroes** (1126—98)**, Ali ben Ragel** (c.1100), Arabic physicians and philosophers further refined art of character judgement in *de Animalibus*.

Book of Splendor, an addition to the Kabala (book of Jewish doctrines) which included a section on physiognomy entitled Secret of Secrets, restatement of *de Animalibus*

Michael Scot, (c.1175—c.1234), physician and astrologer to Emperor Frederick II, wrote the first book entirely devoted to physiognomy, *de Hominis Physiognomia.*

Albertus Magnus (1193—1280, teacher of Thomas Aquinas)**, and Thomas Aquinas** (1225—1274) both wrote theories of physiognomy.

Johanne Reuchlin (1455—1522), translated and commented on Kabala and other Jewish and Arabian works. Shakespeare, Milton, Dryden, Descartes, Spinoza made use of physiognomic theory in many of their works.

Giovani Conte Pico de Mirandola (1463—1494), Italian humanist and philosopher, wrote 900 theses attempting to reconcile Platonism and Christianity. Helped introduce Plato's physiognomic ideas into Rennaissance thought.

Giambattista della Porta, (1538—1615), a brilliant Italian, made the first concerted attempt to synthesize various disciplines in his *Celestial Physiognomy*, making his case for the divine identity, form, and nature of

900 AD

1000 AD

1200 AD

1400 AD

1500 AD

man, utilizing Hippocrates temperament types and Aristotle's comparisons of man and animal features.

1600 AD

Francis Bacon, (1561—1626), refuted the Aristotilian animal/man theory, endeavored to establish a new knowledge in his multiple volume work *de Augmentis*. He used a methodological approach to study form and features.

1700 AD

Peter Camper, (1722—1789), Dutch anatomist, applied objective scientific method into the structure/function inquiry. His work *Comparative Anatomy* served the medical surgical community into the 20th Century.

Johann Kaspar Lavater, (b. circa 1730), German pastor, teacher, poet, and artist undertook to classify facial features, mental abilities and predispositions in his *Essays in Physiognomy* published in 1775. It became a major resource for well over a century. Rejecting astrology, divina-

1800 AD tion, animal images and theories such as temperament types, he applied the scientific approach of painstaking observation, description, and classification. He had articulate, precise descriptions and finely detailed line drawings. His work was translated into several languages, published for a total of 151 editions, the last in 1940.

Phrenology was a bump in the path of physiognomic theory, originated by **Franz Joseph Gall,** (1758—1828), who proposed a theory that the shape and contours of the skull reflected the structure of the brain and that prominences indicated bodily functions, attitudes, and behaviors of a person. Gall's method was scientific observation, and he approached it from a more substantial basis than those who both preceded him and followed him. He also cautioned strongly against placing too much emphasis on any single characteristic, but rather to look at the gestalt and interactions.

His work was further articulated and systematized and unfortunately subverted by a zealous student, **Johann Gaspar Spurzhiem,** who

1900 AD

coined the term "phrenology" and carried the ideas throughout Europe and America. A Scottish lawyer, **George Combe,** carried the banner after Spurzhiem died in 1832, and it was further turned into a sideshow by the **Fowler** brothers and their brother-in-law, **Samuel Wells**. Lorenzo Fowler's daughter, **Jessie Fowler** lent it some academic respectability in the early 20th Century.

Mary Olmstead Stanton published a work in 1913 entitled *The Encyclopedia of Face and Form Reading.* It was a prodigious effort to classify facial features and their meanings. It was marketed as a means to character reading, but carried the prevailing prejudices of that era.

L. Hamilton McCormick published a book in 1920 called*: Characterology: An Exact Science.* He claimed that no other theory integrated physiognomy, phrenology, and pathognomy into a comprehensive science of character.

Dr. Katherine Blackford wrote a set of ten little books on character analysis, published in 1918 containing twenty-three lessons on characterology based on the best that physiognomy and phrenology had to offer. In her book *Analyzing Character* (1925) she lamented, "As a result of our ignorance, great possibilities lie undeveloped in nearly all men."

William H. Sheldon, (1898—1977), psychologist and medical doctor, embarked on a work to further develop a theory of temperament types including the body types associated with each. He exhaustively measured proportions and came up with three basic types (See page 27). His works include *Psychology and the Promethean Will* (1936), *The Varieties of Human Physique* (1940), *The Varieties of Temperament* (1942), *The Varieties of Delinquent Youth* (1949), and *The Atlas of Men* (1945). He carried out his research through a number of universities and hospitals, including conducting innumerable autopsies, meticulously weighing and measuring the organs and body proportions. His considerable accomplishments have been obscured by controversies around him that persist today.

163

1900 AD

Edward Vincent Jones was a Los Angeles jurist in 1910 when he read Blackford's works and was intrigued. He began an independent scientific study to relate a synthesis of characterology, phrenology, and physiognomy to the extensive research in neurology and medicine that was taking place during the first half of the twentieth Century. His thirty-plus years of intense research yielded a body of knowledge he called Personology. It was statistically validated through his Personology Foundation in the 1950's, and claimed to be over ninety-five percent accurate.

A number of students of the Personology Foundation wrote books in the 1950s through the 1970's, but especially notable was Judge Jones partner, **Robert Whiteside**. He and his wife, **Elizabeth Whiteside**, helped develop some of the psychological profiles associated with the personology traits. Whiteside's books had the typical gender biases of the 1940s and '50s.

A number of books written in the twentieth century were compilations and theories based largely on Chinese face reading, Blackford's books, some personology, and Lavater's work. As with all disciplines, each new generation of work is either built on what has gone before or the knowledge is used as a point of reference or contention to springboard into new directions of development and inquiry.

2000 AD

Rose Rosetree appears to have borrowed from many sources as well as developed her own approach and in the 1980s and 90s helped popularize the concept for today's world.

Today, there are many books on the market, taken from a number of sources, including the Chinese tradition, personology, from the Rosetree method, and several others who have developed their own methods and/or have integrated several sources into their own unique amalgam of face reading techniques. The list and availability grows along with the accuracy and depth of information available through face reading.

Trait Readouts

The following traits only encompass those on either end, not the traits that fall in the mid-range.

Maria
- Values (nose)
- Spontaneous (muzzle)
- Determined (chin)
- Probing (eyelids)
- Perfectionism (ears)

Zak
- Probing (eyelids)
- Dramatic (eyebrows)
- Independent (nostrils)
- Accumulates (ears)
- Succinct (upper lip)
- Lenient (eyes)
- Adequate (forehead)

Karl (pg. vi, Acknowledgments)
- Probing (eyelids)
- Doubting (nose tip)
- Succinct (upper lip)
- Determined (chin)
- Risk taking (cheeks)

Olga
- Evaluative (forehead)
- Pragmatic (ears)
- Verbal (upper lip)
- Determined (chin)

Badger (page 6)
- Probing (no eyelids)
- Lenient (wide-set eyes)
- Independent (nostrils)
- Risk taking (cheekbones)
- Perfectionism (ears)

Jessie (page 8)
- Adequate (forehead)
- Risk taking (cheekbones)
- Independent (nostrils)
- Selective (eyebrows)
- Abstract (forehead)
- Perfectionism (ears)
- Generous (bottom lip)

Martin (page 10)
- Cautious (forehead)
- Selective (eyebrows)
- Generous (bottom lip)
- Abstract (forehead)
- Aim-focused (forehead)
- Emotionalism (irises)
- Values nose)

Kurt (page 15)
- Adequate forehead)
- Dramatic (eyebrows)
- Lenient (eyes)
- Metal face
- Dominant (jaws)
- Succinct (upper lip)

Clarence (page 16)
- Adequate (forehead)
- Systematic (eyebrows)
- Independent (nostrils)
- Sensual (lips)
- Abstract (forehead)
- Pragmatic (ears)

165

Trait Readouts continued

Grace (page 21)
- Adequate (forehead)
- Bottom line (eyelids)
- Systematic (eyebrows)
- Opposition (jawline)
- Succinct (upper lip)
- Perfectionism (ears)

Sophia (page 27)
- Adequate (forehead)
- Independent (nostrils)
- Systematic (eyebrows)
- Endomorph body type
- Generous (bottom lip)

Tim (page 134)
- Abstract (forehead)
- Trusting (nose tip)
- Dependent (nostrils)
- Accumulates (ears)

Suggested Reading

The Blank Slate, the Modern Denial of Human Nature, Steven Pinker, 2002

Nature's Message, Bill Whiteside, 2000

Face Language, Robert Whiteside, c.1962

It's All in The Face, Naomi Tickle, 2003

Amazing Face Reading, Mac Fulfer, 1997

The Power of Face Reading, Rose Rosetree, 1998

About Faces, Terry Landau, 1989

Mapping the Mind, Rita Carter, 1998

What the Face Reveals, Henry B. Lin, 1999

The Varieties of Human Physique, William H. Sheldon, 1940

GIVE THE GIFT OF
Faces: What You See is What You Get
TO YOUR FRIENDS AND COLLEAGUES

❏ Yes I want _____ Copies of *Faces: What You See is What You Get* for 16.99 each. Please include $3.95 **shipping and handling** for one book, and $1.95 for each additional book if sent to the same address.

❏ Yes I want information about seminars, training, and presentations.

_____ Books @ 16.99 each $ _____.____

Sales Tax (TX residents only) $1.40/bk $ _____.____

Shipping (see above) $ _____.____

TOTAL $ _____.____

Payment must accompany orders. (TX residents: One book total = $22.34)

Please make your Check or Money Order **payable to Sandra William**s

  Mail this order form and payment to :

  S J Williams, Que Publishing Services

  P. O. Box 24911

  Fort Worth, TX 76124-1911

Name_____

Organization _____

Address_____

City/State/Zip _____

Phone _____

e-mail_____

For Credit Card Orders (Visa, MasterCard, Discover, American Express) Call Connections Bookstore: 817-923-2320